BILLIE HOLIDAY

BILLIE HOLIDAY
THE LAST INTERVIEW
and OTHER CONVERSATIONS

with an introduction by KHANYA MTSHALI

MELVILLE HOUSE
BROOKLYN · LONDON

BILLIE HOLIDAY: THE LAST INTERVIEW
AND OTHER CONVERSATIONS

Copyright © 2019 by Melville House Publishing
First Melville House printing: July 2019

"I'll never sing with a dance band again" © 1939 by *DownBeat Magazine*.
First published in *DownBeat Magazine* on November 1, 1939.

"Don't blame show biz!" © 1947 by *DownBeat Magazine*. First published
in *DownBeat Magazine* on June 4, 1947.

"*MacDougall and Friends*" © 1951 by Canadian Broadcasting Corporation. First
published in *MacDougall and Friends* on August 16, 1952.

"The lost Billie Holiday interview" © 1956 by Gordon Skene and *Past Daily*.
First appeared on The Green Room on KNX radio Los Angeles in September 1956.

"*Voice of America Jazz Hour*" © 1956 by the University of Northern Texas
Music Library, Willis Conover Collection. First appeared on *Voice of America
Jazz Hour* with Willis Conover on March 20, 1956.

"*Night Beat*" © 1956 by the University of Michigan Bentley Historical Library
Mike Wallace papers collection. First appeared on *Night Beat* (Dumont Television)
on November 8, 1956.

"Statement of Mrs. Elanor Gough Mckay, also known as Miss Billie Holiday" ©
1959 by U.S. Immigration and Customs Enforcement. Taken in the office
of the Supervising Custom Agent on January 15, 1959.

"The Last Interview: 'I needed heroin to live'" by Billie Holiday and William Dufty.
First published in *Confidential Magazine* in October 1959.

Every reasonable effort has been made to trace the owners of the copyright
for "The Last Interview: 'I needed heroin to live,'" but this has proved impossible.
The publishers and editors will be glad to receive any information leading to
more complete acknowledgements for subsequent printings of this book.

Melville House Publishing   Suite 2000
        46 John Street   and   16/18 Woodford Road
    Brooklyn, NY 11201   London E7 0HA

mhpbooks.com
@melvillehouse

ISBN: 978-1-61219-674-9
ISBN: 978-1-61219-67-56 (eBook)

Printed in the United States of America
10 9 8 7 6 5 4 3 2 1

A catalog record for this book is available from the Library of Congress.

CONTENTS

INTRODUCTION

KHANYA MTSHALI

Over a montage of photos featuring white crowds gathered under trees bearing the hanged bodies of black men and women, I heard the opening lines to Billie Holiday's "Strange Fruit." At the time, I was sixteen and home alone, watching back-to-back documentaries on TV because I assumed that's what serious and smart adults did in their free time. The name of this particular documentary escapes me, but I do recall feeling briefly disconnected from my mind and body as I listened to this haunting, melodic voice drone over each lyric of this violent southern gothic. Delivered with an intense and stirring moral clarity, something seemed eerily familiar about the violence described by Holiday in this "pastoral scene of the gallant South."

Though my upbringing in post-apartheid South Africa had been an entire world away from Billie Holiday's America, "Strange Fruit" reminded me of the times my grandmother would recount the tyranny of living under the apartheid regime, where she was forced to bury the bodies of school-going children, wake up to the smell of gunpowder and tear gas, and hear about the death of a loved one over the radio. What Holiday created was something akin to a communal obituary for the premature deaths of black people at the hands of white supremacy. "Strange Fruit" may have been a black American meditation on the brutality of racism, but to me, it also came to represent the suffering and survival of all descendants of the African continent.

From that moment on, I decided I needed to hear more of Billie Holiday. I proceeded to download every single song of hers I could find on the free-MP3 platforms of my youth, hating myself for letting her brilliance be filtered through this illicit world of terribly designed websites riddled with computer viruses. I felt guilty for allowing someone of Holiday's stature to fall victim to the post-album, free-for-all mess of early-aughts internet culture, but at least, I selfishly reasoned, I now owned some of her music.

Holiday didn't make too many film appearances, and some of the footage from her TV appearances has been lost, leaving just a trail of audio behind. But as YouTube began to stretch its wings, I searched high and low for anything video-like, stumbling on a clip of hers which struck me as one of her finest performances. In *Symphony in Black: A Rhapsody of Negro Life*, a short musical film directed by Fred Waller and composed by Duke Ellington in 1935, Holiday makes a brief and uncredited cameo. She was just nineteen at the time. The film, which explores the realities of everyday black life in America, splices shots of Ellington's orchestra in performance and ordinary black people working, dancing, and singing. Holiday comes into focus about three minutes in, emerging from the black of the night, and staring into the apartment window of her former beau dancing with his current belle. As her old lover comes out of his apartment building, Holiday throws herself at him, begging for his affections. He, in turn, rejects her advances, and pushes her to the ground.

Dejected, Holiday eventually lifts her face and launches into the opening lines of Ellington's "Saddest Tale":

The saddest tale on land or sea
Was when my man walked out on me

Holiday is captivating in her role as the forlorn lover whose man has moved on while she still mourns their relationship. While other singers delivered unrequited love songs in a direct, one-dimensional way, Holiday layered her performances with high emotional stakes, giving these songs a life-or-death quality. Her appearance in *Symphony in Black* would define her as the unofficial queen of torch songs, typical of the Tin Pan Alley era of the early twentieth century. While these sometimes thin and formulaic songs about romance and heartbreak may have been beneath Holiday's crisp phrasing and horn player's knack for improvisation, she was able to elevate them into dramatic ballads worthy of an imperial romance.

Like many Billie Holiday fans, the more I learned about her personal history, the more protective I got over her legacy—so much so, that I refused to watch Diana Ross's performance in the 1972 film *Lady Sings the Blues*, because I'd read that it depicted her life as a tragic pantomime. Holiday was born Eleanor Fagan Gough (or Elinore Harris, according to some records) on April 7, 1915, in Philadelphia, Pennsylvania. She spent her formative years in Baltimore, Maryland, where she was shuffled between different relatives while her mother struggled to get regular work as a maid. In one of the interviews included here, Holiday claims her father, Clarence Holiday of the Fletcher Henderson Orchestra, became less present in her life after he remarried when she was ten. Around that time, Holiday was reported to have been raped and then sent to Catholic reformatory school for about two years. After leaving with the help of relatives, she moved to New York with her mother, where they began engaging in sex work to make ends meet. Holiday was only fourteen.

As I began writing the introduction for this set of interviews, I worried about falling into the trap of treating Holiday as a symbol for the sordid dangers of celebrity. Any discussion of her life, in my mind, could be used to further myths about her image as a tragic heroine who made sad and soulful music about how life had done her in. Yet it would be disingenuous of me to leave these details out under the rather condescending guise of championing the brilliance of her music—something not even the most contrarian of us could deny. Holiday wasn't one to shy away from being frank about the dire circumstances that she'd lived through.

And so I realized that one cannot write about Billie Holiday without mentioning her drug offenses. In May 1947, law enforcement discovered heroin in her room at the Attucks

Hotel in Philadelphia, where she was due to play with Louis
Armstrong at the Earle Theater. She was sentenced to a year
and a day at the Federal Reformatory for Women in Alderson,
West Virginia. In a 1947 interview Holiday conducted with
DownBeat Magazine just ten days before her hearing at a
Philadelphia federal court, she instructs interviewer Michael
Levin not to blame her troubles on show business. "When
you're writing, straighten them out about my people," she
tells Levin. "Tell 'em I made my mistake but show people
aren't all like that. Whatever I did wrong, nobody else but
me was to blame." Holiday then launches into a critique of
the double standards applied to black people who happened
to make regrettable mistakes in life. "I'm a Negro," she says,
"I've got two strikes against me, and don't you forget it." Yet
Holiday is adamant on the right to be flawed and messed up
while black, going on to say, "I'm proud of those two strikes.
I'm as good as a lot of people of all kind."

When I first came across Holiday's candid discussions
about her struggles with substance abuse, I felt a piercing fa-
miliarity which quickly gave way to an intense shame. In my
early twenties, I came into my own troubles with substance
dependency, and Holiday had become much more to me
than just the gifted vocalist whose chilling protest song about
American racism had moved me as a teenager. I didn't want
to think of myself as the kind of person who found Holiday's
heroin addiction dark and glamorous, or her alcoholism the
true mark of genius. But she was someone I could admire for
trying and failing, and trying and failing to fight and understand her addictions in full view of the public. I realized that
Holiday, like all addicts and addict-adjacents, was a human

being who'd fallen into a habit she couldn't live without. For me, separating Holiday from her addiction would tell addicts, particularly black women addicts, that no matter how talented or beloved they are they'd still fall short of being afforded full humanity. It would seem to cast judgment on those who, like Holiday, discovered the best and worst versions of themselves at the bottom of a bottle, or the sharpest end of a needle. Addiction is lonely, hard, and exhausting, especially for women addicts born poor or working-class, who are rarely given any real shot at redemption. I decided it'd be callous and unhelpful to treat Holiday's addictions as an unnecessary distraction.

In the rest of the 1947 *DownBeat* interview, Holiday not only blames herself for her addictions, but she also displays an allegiance to "show people," or jazz musicians, who she loved and respected deeply. At the time, the jazz world was dealing with a pervasive substance abuse problem, with the likes of Charlie Parker, John Coltrane, and Miles Davis famously becoming hooked on "junk," and nodding off at gigs, or missing them entirely. Holiday, who drank alcohol and smoked marijuana throughout the thirties, was allegedly introduced to opium by her first husband, trombonist Jimmy Monroe, whom she married in 1941 and later divorced in 1947. During their marriage, Holiday had begun an affair with trumpeter Joe Guy, whom she'd later marry in 1951 and divorce in 1956. In the interview, Holiday expresses her devotion to Guy, despite admitting that her manager, Joe Glaser, disapproved of him because he felt Guy had a bad influence on her. But she refuses to make her lover the face of her downfall, even though he was alleged to have supplied her with drugs while they were together.

In his book *Chasing The Scream: The First and Last Days of the War on Drugs*, journalist Johann Hari writes that the Federal Bureau of Narcotics (FBN), led by an ambitious, jazz-loathing man named Harry Anslinger, had started pursuing jazz musicians suspected of drug use. Holiday's profile had risen dramatically after her performance of "Strange Fruit" at the nightclub Café Society in Greenwich Village in 1939. This, according to Hari, made her an attractive target for the FBN. Following her release from the women's reformatory in West Virginia, Holiday made a triumphant comeback at Carnegie Hall on March 27, 1948, where she performed two concerts for a sold-out crowd. Nonetheless, she would struggle to make the same earnings she'd made before prison. Because of her conviction, she'd been stripped of her New York City cabaret card, which prevented her from performing in establishments where liquor was sold—in other words, most of the places where jazz was played.

In January 1949, Holiday was arrested in San Francisco, this time for opium possession. Months later, a jury would drop the charges against her on a technicality issue. Holiday would later tell *Ebony Magazine* in 1949 that she was sick of the "vindictive, hounding, heckling and harassing" of law officials. But as Hari later points out in his book, this increased surveillance did nothing but foster a sense of community within the jazz scene, which collectively came to view law enforcement as the enemy.

Holiday's feelings of camaraderie toward her peers weren't just limited to protecting them from public scrutiny. In a 1956 radio interview for *Voice of America Jazz Hour*, included here, she discusses her music in relation to the musicians who she saw herself as an extension of. She describes her singing style as being a combination of Louis Armstrong, whose improvisational style she admired and emulated, and Bessie Smith, whose big voice and emotional expression she enjoyed.

Armstrong and Holiday, who were both friends and collaborators, were also label mates on Decca Records in the forties, and later Verve in the fifties. In 1947, they performed together in *New Orleans*, a comically ambitious and plotty movie about the Jazz Age as told through a forty-year love story. Holiday's devotion to Satchmo was so strong, that when he was accused of "Tomming" for white audiences, she came to his defense, albeit awkwardly, remarking, "God bless Louis Armstrong! He Toms from the heart!"*

It wasn't just Satchmo who Holiday held in high regard. Lester Young, the tenor sax player who she nicknamed "Prez," was often referred to as Holiday's musical soul mate and best friend. In the *Voice of America* interview, Holiday says that when Young, who gave Holiday the moniker "Lady Day," came onto the scene, his delicate and light tone was regarded as unusual, if not undesirable, for a tenor saxophonist. She claims she was one of the few people to declare his sound brilliant and innovative, foretelling how widely it would be mimicked by his peers.

While Holiday could speak highly of her musical comrades, she could be just as harsh and scathing to those who crossed her. This prickliness is on display in her 1939 interview for *DownBeat Magazine*, straightforwardly titled, "I'll

---

* Terry Teachout, *Pops: A Life of Louis Armstrong* (NY: Houghton Mifflin Harcourt, 2009), 324.

Never Sing with a Dance Band Again." Here she discusses
her time with the big swing bands of the thirties. Holiday
was only twenty-four, which becomes evident in her youth-
fully brash criticisms of legends like Count Basie and Artie
Shaw. With Basie, she accuses him of having "too many guys
behind the scenes who told everybody what to do," though
she does mention getting along with the Count himself, and
the band, swimmingly.

Shaw, on the other hand, gets the shorter end of the
stick. As the interview progresses, we discover that her ill feelings toward him aren't simply because of his "snooty, know-
it-all mannerisms." For an engagement at the Lincoln Hotel
in New York, Shaw allegedly made Holiday wait upstairs by
herself until her number, while the rest of his all-white band
remained on stage. She was also forced to use the freight el-
evator and back door, which contributed to her quitting the
band altogether.

Holiday didn't always answer questions in the greatest
detail, usually opting for concise responses when the opportunity presented itself. But as the lack of nightclub engage-
ments made it difficult for her to make a living, she turned to
the burgeoning world of television, notching up appearances
on shows like ABC's *The Comeback Story* in 1953, and NBC's
The Tonight Show with Steve Allen in 1956. Besides performing,
the aim was to present her as a reformed addict as part of an
effort to get her cabaret license back. In an interview with
journalist and TV personality Mike Wallace for his show
Night Beat in 1956, included here, Holiday reveals how much
she desires a quiet, domestic life, with children in a beautiful home where she'd cook often. Wallace had a reputation

for conducting thorough research on the show's subjects for more revelatory interviews, and elsewhere in the interview, he coyly probes Holiday on her "friendships" with the actor Tallulah Bankhead, actor Charles Laughton, and director and writer Orson Welles, who were all rumored to have had affairs with Lady Day. Holiday appears caught off guard, offering a wishy-washy response before getting into more coherent detail on how she became acquainted with the three Hollywood stars.

Though not all of these interviews will shock or surprise the most ardent Billie Holiday fans, it's exciting to see her discuss her music, life, and dreams without the interference of biographers and writers who, in the efforts to distract from the more depressing chapters of her biography, can drift into a convoluted, over-compensatory academese about her vocal abilities and emotional expression.

In a 1951 CBC radio interview, Holiday explains the origin story behind her playful and soothing number "God Bless the Child," which she wrote with Arthur Herzog, Jr. According to Holiday, the idea for the song came from a disagreement she had with her mother about loaning her some money. Following the spat, Holiday quipped, "That's all right. God bless the child that's got his own," and later decided to turn the argument into a song with her piano player.

Herzog, on the other hand, told a different story. In *Billie Holiday: Wishing on The Moon*, he tells writer Donald Clarke that he'd asked Holiday for an "old-fashioned Southern expression," which he could make a song out of. Stumped, Holiday allegedly couldn't come up with anything. She eventually began recounting a story about her mother wanting some money from her, to which she said in a huff, "God bless the child that's got his own." Herzog said he decided to use the line as the basis of the song, giving Holiday half of the songwriting credits so she'd be incentivized to record it. He went on to state that Holiday had "never written a line of words or music." Clarke appears to side with Herzog's retelling of events, writing that Holiday's claims about "God Bless the Child," which also feature in her memoir, *Lady Sings the Blues*, couldn't be trusted since the book, ghostwritten by William Dufty, was "hopelessly unreliable."

The veracity of *Lady Sings the Blues* has been questioned because it was wholly written by Dufty, based on his interviews of Holiday (a fact Holiday confirms in these pages in her 1956 interview with George Walsh for KNX radio's *The Green Room*). In *If You Can't be Free, be a Mystery: In Search of Billie Holiday*, scholar and academic Farah Jasmine Griffin, argues for a more complex reading of *Lady Sings the Blues*, acknowledging how it "establish[ed] myths on Holiday," but also recognizing how much the book wanted to challenge incorrect narratives on Lady Day. Anthropologist and jazz scholar John Szwed argues in his 2015 book, *Billie Holiday: The Musician and the Myth*, that the memoir should be treated "as a form of autobiographical fiction," because even though it contained "fabrications and misrememberings," most of the important sources came from "newspaper and magazine interviews with Holiday."

Regardless of where one stands in relation to *Lady Sings the Blues*, Herzog's dismissive attitude toward Holiday's ability to write songs, and Clarke's automatic support of that dismissal, brings to mind a history of white jazz men having little regard for the intelligence and technical capabilities of black jazz musicians. Throughout her career, Holiday had been credited with writing eighteen songs, some of which include classics like "Billie's Blues," "Fine and Mellow," "Don't Explain," and "Lady Sings the Blues." Had she been surrounded by men who thought more of her innate and intuitive grasp of song structure, phrasing, and melody, who knows what sort of material she could've produced?

When Holiday talks about her repertoire, she comes across as bashful and embarrassed, admitting to disliking some of her records in the 1956 *Green Room* interview. Curiously, the segment never aired because Holiday was thought to sound like she was under the influence. When I listened to the audio, I did notice her speaking more slowly than usual. But overall, she sounded cogent (though it is quite possible for some people to be lucid on a substance). Perhaps the refusal to air the interview had more to do with the fear that she was falling off the wagon again.

Holiday cites "Deep Song" and "You're My Thrill," among others, as the songs she liked the most from her discography. The latter is a moody and wistful song about the intensity of infatuation, and a shining testament to the way Holiday was able to convey the emotional ebb and flow of romantic relationships in a seemingly basic love song. Being in love is not an easy and ideal experience, she seems to say. Instead, it can be terrifying, obsessive, manic, and all-consuming, with little to no payoff. Holiday intersperses the number with a hum that sounds like the grim reaper's lullaby, managing to be soothing, sensual, and thrilling against the operatic string arrangement.

Arguably, the most revealing interview takes place between Holiday and a "Supervising Custom Agent" in New York on January 15, 1959—five months before her death. In an interesting intersection of feminist politics, her lawyer in the interrogation room happens to be Florynce Kennedy, future women's liberation leader and pro-choice advocate, who went on to be the executor of Holiday's estate. As the questioning begins, Lady Day is informed that, on a recent trip to Europe, she violated a law so new neither she nor her attorney knew about it: It required her to declare her narcotic offences not only upon departure as usual (which Holiday had done) but also upon return (the new part Holiday hadn't known to do). She appears bewildered and frustrated throughout the interrogation, repeating that her team hadn't informed her about the law. Though she's polite and restrained throughout the process, one senses how worn out she feels. She concludes the interview by making a broader comment about being an addict in the criminal justice system, proclaiming that "once you get in trouble for narcotics, it's the end."

This quiet but gracious acceptance of her fate would come through in her final television performance in February 1959 on the British variety show, *Chelsea at Nine*, performed at the Chelsea Palace Theatre for Granada TV. Holiday, who looked less gaunt in comparison to her appearances in 1958, wore a knee-length glitter dress and long diamond chandelier earrings with her hair slicked back into a ponytail. In this particular performance, she is more understated than usual, with her arm gestures resembling more of a stride than the tightly controlled rock of her youth. Her voice is coarser and shakier, and her phrasing fuzzier and slower, giving her already distinctive voice an unusual layer of character.

In hindsight, it's easy to view this recital with more finality and sorrow, given how close Holiday was to her own death. But her renditions of "I Love You Porgy" and "Please Don't Talk About Me When I'm Gone" are slower and more pronounced, sung with the same heart and wit, but with an additional measure of maturity and experience. In this version of "Strange Fruit," arguably Holiday's best, it sounds like she's delivering a war cry from the underworld, with her gravelly voice partnering well with her unhinged approach to singing the song's notes. Vocally, it's a messy and bizarre performance, but somehow it gives the number more emotional depth and gravitas.

The last interview, "I Needed Heroin to Live," reads like a fatalistic, editorialized monologue. Published posthumously, Holiday was alleged to have dictated these final words to William Dufty, the ghostwriter of her *Lady Sings the Blues*, from her bed at New York's Metropolitan Hospital, where she died on July 17, 1959, with $750 strapped to her leg and seventy cents in her bank account. In the interview, Holiday laments the tabloids which sensationalized her drug use, criticizes the music people who took advantage of her, berates America for its treatment of black people, and bemoans the bad hand she'd been dealt in life. Her understanding of addiction seems more considered, even ahead of her time, as she calls for professionals to see "the 'human' side of the drug addict." Much like *Lady Sings the Blues*, the interview does bring up issues of authorship and reliability, because we don't know how much of the piece came from Holiday or Dufty.

But it does capture an idea, which nonaddicts might struggle to understand: addiction brings about turmoil, pain, and loss, but it can also be something in which the addict finds joy and reprieve. What Holiday shows, as she had in some of her previous interviews, is a defiant refusal to simply cast regret over her actions. Here, she seems to speak for addicts who have experienced a range of conflicting emotions around substance abuse. Her underlying sentiment aligns with Holiday's sensibility, perfectly captured in the line, "I hold no regrets and I carry no shame."

There's no way of talking about Billie Holiday without acknowledging the events that drove her to self-destruction. Yet what these interviews seem to suggest is that more than anybody else, Holiday was able to hold conflicting and unresolved feelings about how her life ended up. Yes, it was tragic, but it was her tragedy to bear. Yes, she inflicted pain on herself, but she was able to make art from it. For those of us who feel like she was cheated out of so much, it can be difficult to be at peace with this. But Lady Day seemed to know better.

BILLIE HOLIDAY

BILLIE HOLIDAY: "I'LL NEVER SING WITH A DANCE BAND AGAIN"

BY DAVE DEXTER, JR.
DOWNBEAT MAGAZINE
NOVEMBER 1, 1939

CHICAGO—You sit with Billie Holiday and watch her smoke cigarettes chain fashion. The first thing that strikes you is her frankness.

"I'll never sing with a dance band again," she tells you. "Because it never works out right for me. They wonder why I left Count Basie, and why I left Artie Shaw. Well I'll tell you why—and I've never told this before.

"Basie had too many managers—too many guys behind the scenes who told everybody what to do. The Count and I got along fine. And the boys in the band were wonderful all the time. But it was this and that, all the time, and I got fed up with it. Basie didn't fire me; I gave him my notice."

BAD KICKS WITH SHAW

"Artie Shaw was a lot worse. I had known him a long time, when he was strictly from hunger around New York, long before he got a band. At first we worked together okay, then his managers started belly-aching. Pretty soon it got so I would sing just two numbers a night. When I wasn't singing, I had to stay backstage. Artie wouldn't let me sit out front with the band. Last year when we were at the Lincoln Hotel the hotel management told me I had to use the back door. That was all right. But I had to ride up and down in the freight elevators, and every night Artie made me stay upstairs in a little room without a radio or anything all the time.

"Finally it got so I would stay up there, all by myself, reading everything I could get my hands on, from 10 o'clock to nearly 2 in the morning, going downstairs to sing just one or two numbers. Then one night we had an airshot. Artie said he couldn't let me sing. I was always given two shots on each program. The real trouble was this—Shaw wanted to sign me to a five-year contract and when I refused, it burned him. He was jealous of the applause I got when I made one of my few appearances with the band each night."

NEVER PAID FOR RECORD

You ask Billie why she didn't make more records with Shaw. You remember that the only side she made, on Bluebird, was a thing titled "Any Old Time" and was really wonderful.

"That's a laugh," she answers. "Artie never paid me for that record. Just before it came out I simply got enough of Artie's snooty, know-it-all mannerisms, and the outrageous behavior of his managers, and left the band. I guess Artie forgot about 'Any Old Time.' I know he never paid me. With Basie I got $70 a week—with Artie I got $65. When I make my own records I get $150. That's another reason I left Shaw.

"One afternoon we were driving along in Artie's car to a

one-night stand. We passed an old man on the road who had a beard. I asked Artie if he had ever worn a beard, and that I'd bet he sure'd look funny if he wore one.

"Chuck Petersen, George Arus, Les Jenkins, and a couple of other boys in the band were also in the car. So we were all surprised when Artie said 'I used to wear a beard all the time—when I was farming my own farm a few years back.' I asked Artie if he looked good or bad with a beard—and I was just joking, you know, to make conversation on a long drive.

"'Indeed I did look fine with a beard,' Artie said. 'I looked exactly like Jesus Christ did when he was young.'"

Billie slapped her pudgy thigh, lighted another cigarette, and continued.

GAVE HIM A NAME

You should have heard the boys and me roar at that. We got a bang out of it. Artie looked mad, because he had been serious. So I said, 'We'll just call you Jesus Christ, King of the Clarinet, and his Band.'

"Now here's the payoff—the story got out around Boston and even today, we hear a lot of the musicians refer to Artie as 'Jesus Christ and his Clarinet'."

You figure you've heard enough dirt about the pitfalls of a young girl with a dance band and you ask Billie to tell you something about herself. She comes through with the word that she is Baltimore born, and that she got her first job when she was 14 years old, after she and her mother moved to New York.

BILLIE GETS DESPERATE

"This is the truth. Mother and I were starving. It was cold. Father had left us and remarried when I was 10. Mother was a housemaid and couldn't find work. I tried scrubbing floors, too, but I just couldn't do it."

"We lived on 145th Street near Seventh Avenue. One day we were so hungry we could barely breathe. I started out the door. It was cold as all-hell and I walked from 145th to 133rd down Seventh Avenue, going in every joint trying to find work. Finally, I got so desperate I stopped in the Log Cabin Club, run by Jerry Preston. I told him I wanted a drink. I didn't have a dime. But I ordered gin (it was my first drink—I didn't know gin from wine) and gulped it down. I asked Preston for a job . . . told him I was a dancer. He said to dance. I tried it. He said I stunk. I told him I could sing. He said sing. Over in the corner was an old guy playing a piano. He struck 'Travelin' and I sang. The customers stopped drinking. They turned around and watched. The pianist, Dick Wilson, swung into 'Body and Soul.' Jeez, you should have seen those people—all of them started crying. Preston came over, shook his head and said 'Kid, you win.' That's how I got my start."

GOODMAN USES HER

"First thing I did was get a sandwich. I gulped it down. Believe me—the crowd gave me $18 in tips. I ran out the door. Bought a whole chicken. Ran up Seventh Avenue to my home. Mother and I ate that night—and we have been eating pretty well since."

Benny Goodman used Billie on a record (Columbia) of "My Mother's Son in Law" when Teagarden, Krupa and others were in his recording band—before he really organized his present combo. The disc is an item today, not only because of the fine instrumental work, but because it was Holiday's first side. She was pretty lousy. You tell her so and she grins. "But I was only 15 then," she said, "And I was scared as the devil."

SHE DOESN'T SING

You tell Billie you think you've got enough dope for a little story, but that one thing worries you. That is—why does she sing like she does—what's behind it?

"Look Dex," Billie answers. "I don't think I'm singing. I feel like I am playing a horn. I try to improvise like Les Young, like Louie Armstrong, or someone else I admire. What comes out is what I feel. I hate straight singing. I have to change a tune to my own way of doing it. That's all I know."

SAD LOVE LIFE

You ask her one more thing, recalling how at various times Billie has been reported ready to marry. She shows her frankness again. "I've loved three men," she tells you. "One was a Marion Scott, when I was a kid. He works for the post office now. The other was Freddie Green, Basie's guitar man. But Freddie's first wife is dead and he has two children and somehow it didn't work out. The third was Sonny White, the pianist, but like me, he lives with his mother and our plans for marriage didn't jell. That's all."

Billie says she isn't satisfied now. She wants to get somewhere. Maybe on the stage. She wants to make money—a lot of it. She wants to buy a big home for her mother. She doesn't expect any happiness—she is used to taking hard knocks, tough breaks. And she admits she is envious of Maxine Sullivan and other colored singers who have gotten so much farther ahead than she. Someday, she thinks, she'll get a real break. But she's not very optimistic about it. Billie Holiday is convinced the future will be as unglamorous and unprofitable as her past.

"DON'T BLAME SHOW BIZ!"

BY MICHAEL LEVIN
DOWNBEAT MAGAZINE
JUNE 4, 1947

BULLETIN—At press time, Billie Holiday was released on $1,000 bail by U.S. Commissioner Norman J. Griffith in Philadelphia to return for further hearing today, June 4. *DownBeat* learned from an unimpeachable source that in all probability charges would not be pressed against her, she would be allowed to finish out her present run at the Club 18 in New York and other work presently contracted, and then would probably go to Lexington, Ky., for medical treatment of some months' duration.

NEW YORK—"When you're writing, straighten them out about my people. Tell 'em I made my mistake but show people aren't all like that. Whatever I did wrong, nobody else but me was to blame—and show people aren't wrong."

That's what Billie Holiday said 10 days ago before arraignment in Philadelphia federal court on charges of possessing heroin in her Attucks hotel room there.

"I'm not offering an alibi, I'm not singing the blues. Things weren't easy. There were a lot of things I didn't have when I was a kid. My mother died 18 months ago, the only relative I had in the world. I guess I flipped, run through more than $100,000 since then.

"But I was trying to go straight. It just seems as though I have a jinx over me. I was with Count Basie when things were really rough, then I had a fight with John Hammond and got fired. I stuck with Artie Shaw through that Southern road tour; we got back to New York and they had to let me go. It's been one thing after another.

"This year I made a picture, my records were really selling, it was going to be my time."

SAYS SHE'S THROUGH

"Now it looks finished. I'm through—at least for a while. After all this is over, maybe I'll go to Europe, perhaps Paris, and try to start all over. Sure, I know about Gene Krupa—but don't forget he's white and I'm a Negro. I've got two strikes against me, and don't you forget it.

"I'm proud of those two strikes. I'm as good as a lot of people of all kinds—I'm proud I'm a Negro. And you know the funniest thing: the people that are going to be the hardest on me will be my own race. Look what they did to Billy Eckstine for three weeks in two of the big Negro papers—and you know that was a frame-up.

"You know, I just spent $3,000 of my own money taking the cure for three weeks. Maybe I was a fool to do it. It put me on record. They may have suspected before, but they were never sure of it. Now the federal people tell me they may send me away for another cure—and they never tell you how long it will be.

"Just when things were going to be so big and I was trying so hard to straighten myself out. Funny, isn't it?"

TUCKER NOT INVOLVED

"Bobby Tucker? My piano player? Baby, the strongest thing he ever had in his life was a Camel cigarette. Believe me he is the most innocent thing that ever was. [Editor's Note: Tucker has been released due to lack of evidence.]

"You know what actually happened? I was coming back to the hotel and we noticed a lot of people around it, and my driver, Bill, said it looked like it had been raided. I told him he was crazy, but we parked by the side of the hotel, and he went up to see what was going on. He saw some agents and came running back to the car. Evidently he had one offense against him for something and they had told him he would lose his car if he did anything else. Well, he started the car like it was a jackrabbit, and we tore by a couple of policemen on the sidewalk.

"I heard a couple of sounds like shots, and I asked him and he said yes, they were shots but that he was afraid to stop, he didn't know what was going on. So we came back to New York City.

"Don't believe that business about our trying to run down an agent. Were we driving over the sidewalk? You know another funny thing: one of those officers mixed up in the case is Lt. Anderson, Marian Anderson's nephew."

HUSBAND HELD

"They're sitting on my Joe Guy downtown right now. They're holding him on $3,000 bail, claim he was mixed up with some of the stuff they found there. Joe's been a headstrong boy. When I first knew him, he was just playing horn for Lucky Millinder. I gave him a lot of clothes and a band. Guess it turned his head, he ran through $35,000 with the band and nothing ever happened.

"But don't let anyone tell you it's his fault. My manager Joe Glaser hates him, says he's responsible for everything that has happened to me. Don't you believe it. I'm grown-up. I knew what I was doing. Joe may have done things he shouldn't, but I did them of my own accord, too. And I never tried to influence anybody else or do anything to hurt anyone. Joe didn't make it any easier for me at times—but then I haven't been an easy gal, either.

"I've made lots of enemies, too. Singing that 'Strange Fruit' hasn't helped any, you know. I was doing it at the Earle (Philadelphia) 'til they made me stop. Tonight they're already talking about me. When I did 'The Man I Love' (at NYC's Club 18), I heard some woman say, 'Hear he's in the jug downtown.'"

WON'T DIVULGE INFO

"Jimmy Asendio? They grabbed him for bringing some stuff wrapped in a stocking he said was mine. Actually what they want me and Joe to do is tell them where—and that is something I would never be sure about. I'm just not cut out for that.

"Of course my singing was never better because of it. I was unhappy and a Negro and a lot of other things. But that was still no excuse—you don't have to tell me that. It's just wrong somehow that it happened when I was trying to turn around.

"I guess *DownBeat* is going to chew me to shreds like the papers are doing. Ned Williams has known me ever since I was a little girl—'bout as old as that 14-year-old picture of me they used in the papers. My eyebrows were all off 'cause I tried to shape 'em and took half of one off by mistake. I never won the *DownBeat* poll. Guess I never will now.

"Don't forget, though. I just want to be straight with people, not have their sympathy. And remember, nobody else in show business has made as many mistakes as me."

MACDOUGALL AND FRIENDS

INTERVIEW WITH DICK MACDOUGALL
AUGUST 16, 1952

DICK MACDOUGAL: My name is Dick MacDougall, and here's my friend.

[*"Billie's Blues" ("I Love My Man") plays in the intro.*]

MACDOUGAL: My friend today is a gal who has been singing jazz for a good many years now, long enough to earn for herself the title of world's greatest jazz vocalist, Miss Billie Holiday. Billie, just when that record was playing, you said something that quite amazed me. How old were you when that record was made?

BILLIE HOLIDAY: Well, Dick, I was exactly fourteen years old and on top of that, I wrote it.

MACDOUGAL: Really, at fourteen years old?

HOLIDAY: That's right. I was inspired from Miss Bessie Smith. She used to be a friend of my mother's, and I used to listen to her records and I'd say I'm going to write a song and that's what happened.

MACDOUGAL: That's a wonderful thing, too. I was going to ask you, you know, so many times these days, when you talk to vocalists and instrumentalists, they say well, I dug Billie ten to twelve years ago and she's my gal.

HOLIDAY: Really?

MACDOUGAL: Yeah.

HOLIDAY: That's wonderful.

MACDOUGAL: So it's interesting to hear that you dug someone even before that, and it was Bessie Smith.

HOLIDAY: Oh, Bessie Smith and Louis Armstrong was my world.

MACDOUGAL: Well, who would you say of the current crop, Billie, in the world of entertainers, is your boy right now?

HOLIDAY: Well, I like Billy Eckstine's singing very much, sweet songs. But Pops—Louis Armstrong—I'll never get over him, that's all.

MACDOUGAL: That's a wonderful thing, too, you know. And here we have Billy Eckstine in Toronto this week, and Billie Holiday.

HOLIDAY: Yes, I heard Billy opened here.

MACDOUGAL: Yes, Billy's at the casino; you're at the Colonial. So in a couple of blocks there, in the middle of the city of Toronto, there's entertainment galore for anyone. Tell us something, Billie, about the background that brought about your interest in jazz back in the old days.

HOLIDAY: Well, the only thing I can tell you, when I was a little girl, I used to run errands, and I was very, very . . . commercial. You had to give me a nickel, you couldn't give me two pennies.

MACDOUGAL: No.

HOLIDAY: But, there was a lady on the corner that had a record machine. And I could hear Louis Armstrong and Bessie Smith, and so I didn't charge her anything!

MACDOUGAL: That was it?

HOLIDAY: That's all. [*laughs*]

MACDOUGAL: You've got to goin', huh?

HOLIDAY: And John Hammond, you've probably heard of him.

MACDOUGAL: Ah, yes. He's the well-known critic.

HOLIDAY: And Benny Goodman and Mildred Bailey and her

husband.* They used to come up to hear me in Harlem, and that's how I slowly got started.

MACDOUGAL: Well, now, wait a minute; it's quite a jump from, I believe your hometown is Rochester, isn't it?

HOLIDAY: Baltimore, Maryland!

MACDOUGAL: Baltimore, is it? Oh, well, it's still quite a hop from Baltimore to New York.

HOLIDAY: Messing me up! Well, it was a jump. And it was 133rd Street. And at that time, 133rd Street was like 52nd Street was when it was jumping.

MACDOUGAL: That was the hive.

HOLIDAY: Yeah, they had the clubs, you know, the Nest Club, the Log Cabin—that's where I was—the Stables. It was like 52nd, and that's where I met Mr. Hammond and Mildred Bailey, Benny Goodman, Teddy Wilson . . .

MACDOUGAL: Who was it that brought about the job you did with Artie Shaw in the old days, you remember?

HOLIDAY: Well, Artie Shaw.

MACDOUGAL: Himself.

* Bailey was married to jazz vibraphonist and bandleader Red Norvo.

HOLIDAY: He came up to hear me. And he used to like to come up and sit in with the guys, you know. And he'd come up and sit in and maybe we'd play 'til eight, nine o'clock next morning. And I'd sing. And he asked me do I want a job, and he's working in Roseland in Boston. So I says, "Yeah, I want a job. What kind of job is it?" I thought it was a nightclub. When I found out it was a dance hall I almost died because I'd never worked in such a big place!

MACDOUGAL: I often look back on the old days and I suppose you do, too, the days when, let's see, Ella Fitzgerald with Chick Webb—

HOLIDAY: She was one block from me at the time.

MACDOUGAL: Just one block, was it?

HOLIDAY: Yeah, she was in a small club with Chick at the same time.

MACDOUGAL: And then there was Mildred Bailey with Red Norvo.

HOLIDAY: That's right.

MACDOUGAL: And, of course, you with Artie Shaw. Those were the good old days of big band jazz. You ever wonder whatever happened to those days, Billie?

HOLIDAY: [*sighs*] Yes, I do. I think they were the good days. We used to think we were scufflin' then. [*laughs*]

MACDOUGAL: Yeah, well, isn't that the truth? But you, like a lot of other people, wish they'd certainly get back again. Tell us something about that wonderful, wonderful series of recordings you did on the Columbia label, you know, with Benny Goodman and Teddy Wilson and Roy Eldridge, "Miss Brown To You" and stuff like that.

HOLIDAY: Well, those things were just so impromptu, um—I'll tell you about one date, when we did "Easy Living," "What A Little Moonlight Can Do," uh, "If You Were Mine" . . . I was with Count Basie up in Albany, New York. And we had the worst bus in the world! And we finally made it into New York, I never will know how. It was so glassy on the road; the bus spinned around about eight times. We made it. And we go right in, nobody washed their face or anything, and we make eight sides!

MACDOUGAL: Just like that.

HOLIDAY: The good days! [*laughs*]

MACDOUGAL: And what wonderful sides they were, too. They're not exactly collectors' items today because they've been released and reissued so many, many times, everybody buys them, but they're records that are going to be cherished, I think, by jazz fans for the next, well, you name it, number of years. Eh, talking about those old Columbia sides reminds me of a thing that is not exactly the latest thing you ever did, but it's certainly one that's very popular around here, especially, I think, since you've been doing some work at the Colonial, and this is a popular tune right in town. This is your great Decca recording of "You're My Thrill."

[*song plays*]

MACDOUGAL: "You're My Thrill," Billie Holiday. I hope you'll excuse me mentioning all the different record labels but you're something like Erroll Garner, you've been on so many of them.

[*Holiday laughs*]

MACDOUGAL: I recall another one about 1944–45 that you did with Paul Whiteman.

HOLIDAY: Well, that's another story. At the time, I was contracted to Columbia and I was on the coast, and Mr. Whiteman approached me and he wanted me to make "Trav'lin Light" with him. And, uh, Jimmy—oh, I can't think of Jimmy's last name.* Anyway, he wrote it. He was arranging for Mr. Whiteman. So he says, "Nobody in the world can sing this but you." So I said, "Well, I can't do it. I'm under contract at Columbia." So he says, "Well . . ." So I said, "I'll tell you what; I got a pet name." I said, "If you don't use my name, there's nothing they can do." So we used "Lady Day," which is my pet name—

---

* "Trav'lin Light" was written by Trummy Young and Jimmy Mundy, with lyrics by Johnny Mercer.

MACDOUGAL: Sure.

HOLIDAY: —and we made the record, and there was nothing they could do about it. [*laughs*]

MACDOUGAL: I don't suppose for one minute they thought they could fool anybody, though, with "Lady Day."

HOLIDAY: Oh no, there was a lot of arguments and bets made—"Don't tell me that's Billie Holiday, I know!" [*laughs*]

MACDOUGAL: The guys used to say, "This is a new girl that Capitol just discovered, sounds exactly like Billie Holiday." I know; I lost a bet like that myself once. What about the current recording activities, Billie? What are you doing these days?

HOLIDAY: Well, I'm with Norman Granz now at the jazz philharmonic and just made twenty-two sides with a hometown boy, Oscar Peterson.

MACDOUGAL: Well, nearly, he's actually from Montreal, but he's done a lot of work around here.

HOLIDAY: I know. Still Canada.

[*both laugh*]

HOLIDAY: I think he's wonderful.

MACDOUGAL: He certainly is. Was Oscar on all these things?

HOLIDAY: Yes. We had Ray Brown, Flip Philips, and oh, we had about eight guys, I can't call up the names just now . . .

MACDOUGAL: All the boys, all Norman's flock. It would be kind of nice, you know, if he got that string section he used with Charlie Parker on those Parker with Strings records and put them behind you on a couple of them.

HOLIDAY: Well, we're going to do that. We're going to make some albums like, A Salute to Jerome Kern, Salute to George Gershwin. You know, like that.

MACDOUGAL: Should be wonderful. What else are you doing besides the records and touring around the spots?

HOLIDAY: Well, when we leave here we go to Montreal and then Atlantic City, and the twelfth of October my dream is supposed to come true. I'm going to Europe.

MACDOUGAL: Really? For one of those, uh—

HOLIDAY: I hope. I don't believe it. I still got my fingers crossed.

MACDOUGAL: Say, they're having hassles over there, too, now, you know, with American talent playing the Palladium—is that where you're going, the Palladium? Or are you staying in France, in Germany, or something?

HOLIDAY: We start off in Paris, I think.

MACDOUGAL: Oh, well, I think you should do wonderfully over there.

HOLIDAY: I just don't believe anything until it happens. [*laughs*]

MACDOUGAL: Oh, you've never been there?

HOLIDAY: No. I've always wanted to go.

MACDOUGAL: Oh, well! That'll be a trip and a half. How about the current tunes, Billie? I notice that you don't go much for the, at least you don't sing many of the, new ones.

HOLIDAY: Well, I really don't think they're writing nothing. [*both laugh*] Maybe I should've said that!

MACDOUGAL: You should've said that at first, yeah—they're not writing anything.

HOLIDAY: No, I mean, if you notice, all the artists are doing are bringing back all the old tunes.

MACDOUGAL: That's quite true.

HOLIDAY: There's really nothing happening, I mean, with the tunes today. You just can't get into 'em. You can't feel 'em. Unless you do novelty things—they write cute novelty things. But I don't sing novelty. So there's nothing happening for me.

MACDOUGAL: Well, it's a good thing you don't. This trueness to the blues that you achieve, I think, is achieved by you and you alone in the particular field. It's wonderful to think, too, that—

HOLIDAY: Well, I hope the songwriters listening are not angry with me for saying that, but, um, the things that I sing have to have something to do with me and my life, and my friends' lives, and . . . it has to have a meaning, you know? The things they're writing today, nothing's happening.

MACDOUGAL: Well, isn't that true of—

HOLIDAY: So I can't feel it.

MACDOUGAL: —isn't that true of every singer? I mean, to project, to be able to get across the feeling, you must have lived some of these things or feel it.

HOLIDAY: Well, a lot of them can feel the novelty things! I can't.

[*both laugh*]

MACDOUGAL: You can't feel all of those guitars and the "How High the Moons" and one thing or another? Oh, that's wonderful. You know, this freshness and stimulation that comes about listening to you and, for instance, Teddy Wilson, on some of those old Columbia things, is something I'm sure that will not exist five or six or ten years from today with some of the pop vocalists.

HOLIDAY: And we had no music.

MACDOUGAL: You had no music?

HOLIDAY: Had no rehearsals.

MACDOUGAL: Oh, you're speaking now of these old Columbia sessions with Benny and the boys . . .

HOLIDAY: That's right. You just make a four bar introduction and you go into it.

MACDOUGAL: Ah, but now—

HOLIDAY: And you better make it.

MACDOUGAL: But Billie, now we have producers and things, you know?

[*both laugh*]

HOLIDAY: That's right, and timing.

MACDOUGAL: Well, Billie, I want to thank you very much for dropping in this evening. It really has been a pleasure talking about jazz to someone who has been an important part of it for so many years.

THE LOST BILLIE HOLIDAY INTERVIEW

INTERVIEW WITH GEORGE WALSH
THE GREEN ROOM ON KNX RADIO LOS ANGELES
SEPTEMBER 1956

Editor's note: Concerned that Holiday's manner of speaking in this interview indicated she was under the influence, station management subsequently decided not to air this pre-recorded interview. It went unheard for nearly sixty years, until musician and archivist Gordon Skene uncovered it and posted it on his Past Daily website in 2015.

GEORGE WALSH: Our special *Green Room* guest this afternoon is Mademoiselle Billie Holiday, recording artist for Clef Records. Good afternoon, Mademoiselle Holiday.

BILLIE HOLIDAY: Hello, George.

WALSH: I might add that it is the most pleasant experience, to see that you are as personable in person as you are on your famous recordings.

HOLIDAY: Thank you.

WALSH: We always like to ask our guests a question, and we like to compare their answers. Billie, I wonder if you could answer for us: What is jazz?

HOLIDAY: Well, to me, jazz is good music and a good feeling. And I'd like to say that everybody can't play jazz, and no one person originated it. No one person, uh, created it. I think, uh, you just have to have it in you . . .

WALSH: Are you concur—

HOLIDAY: You have to *feel* it, in other words.

WALSH: You concur with our other guests thus far, then, that jazz must be tied in pretty closely with improvising.

HOLIDAY: That's right.

WALSH: I understand, Billie, that you have, uh, enlarged your scope of talents, not only to include fine singing, but you've also written a book called *Lady Sings the Blues*. I understand, too, that it's a bestseller.

HOLIDAY: Yes, I'm very happy about it, and gee whiz, we tried to get it in, out here in LA, and it was all sold out, and in Chicago and New York, and they're making up some new ones.

WALSH: You mean you couldn't buy a copy of your own book?

HOLIDAY: I never read it yet. [*laughs*] Any one I get, my friends take it away from me.

WALSH: I'll bet they take it away autographed, too. Did you, uh, actually write the book, or did you hire a writer to write it for you?

HOLIDAY: No, I, uh, a friend of mine, um, Dufty* is his name, he's a coeditor for the *Post* in New York, the *Post* newspaper and, um—well, to make a long story short, my husband, one night we were talking, and people had been writing things about me and gettin' them all wrong and all screwed up—I won't mention the newspapers or the magazines, bless 'em [*laughs*]—so my husband said, "Why don't you write a book and tell your side?" So I went to Bill, and he got the typewriter, and it took us about two, three months, and . . . I just told him, and he wrote. That's how the book came about.

WALSH: You make it sound so simple, and I'm sure it was a lot of work and a lot of inspiration. Billie, you've described jazz as, somewhat, as being a good feeling. Do you have any particular recordings of your own that had this good feeling when you made them?

HOLIDAY: Um, yeah. I . . . I don't like very many of my records though, because there's always something I should'a

---

* William Dufty (1916–2002) was a musician, labor activist, and newspaperman who, in addition to ghostwriting *Lady Sings the Blues*, wrote numerous books, including the 1975 bestseller *Sugar Blues*, which he coauthored with his wife, the actor Gloria Swanson.

did, some note that should'a been, some word I should'a said. [*laughs*] I should of slowed down or went faster. But, ah, I . . . I—yeah. I like other people's records, Duke Ellington, I'm crazy about Ella and Louis Armstrong. They're my favorites. But my records . . . I don't know. [*laughs*]

WALSH: Well, I think you're being too critical [*laughs*] of your own recordings, Billie. I think that they're certainly most enjoyable to listen to, despite the fact that you wish you had another chance at them.

Billie, what is new? What's, what are your plans for the immediate future?

HOLIDAY: Well, when we leave here we go to Honolulu, and then we go to—where do we go?

MAN OFF MIC: Camden, New Jersey

HOLIDAY: Oh, that's right. We have a concert—isn't that an outdoor fair or something? First it's a concert outdoors, and then we go to Camden, New Jersey, and then we go to Europe.

WALSH: Well, is this a vacation trip to Europe or—

HOLIDAY: No, honey, no vacations. All work.

WALSH: Well, that's wonderful, that's—

HOLIDAY: I vacation while I work, you know. [*laughs*]

WALSH: Well, I know you like to sing, because you couldn't sing so well if you didn't like it. Do you like to do anything else particularly?

HOLIDAY: Well, I tried to learn to play golf; my husband's a golf fiend and . . . but I like, uh, the other thing that he likes—that's fishing. But the only thing I like about it is to sit in the boat and eat the hotdogs and drink beer and scream when he catches a fish.

WALSH: And you hope that you don't catch any fish. [*they laugh*]

HOLIDAY: No, they wiggle too much! I'm afraid to take them off the hook. [*laughs*]

WALSH: Well, I've got to ask you the perennial question then, Mademoiselle

HOLIDAY: Who puts the worm on the hook?

HOLIDAY: My husband.

WALSH: He baits your hook for you.

HOLIDAY: Sure, I'm afraid of them. They wiggle.

WALSH: You're afraid of everything that wiggles.

HOLIDAY: [*laughs*] I don't like 'em!

WALSH: Well, did he ever introduce you to the type of bait that is actually mechanical, a little silver spoon—

HOLIDAY: Yes! And, uh, he never introduced me, but he bought this little kit and—nosy me—I went and opened it, to see what was inside, and those things are so real! It scared me to death! I must have threw it a mile! [*laughs*]

WALSH: You thought he brought home a boxful of bugs?

HOLIDAY: [*laughing*] I certainly did.

WALSH: Well, that's wonderful. And . . . and where is your favorite fishing spot?

HOLIDAY: Well, we've been all over Canada and Detroit, out here . . . And in Miami, he went out in the Everglades.

WALSH: To go fishing?

HOLIDAY: And in a little boat, and went over an alligator's back, and a storm came up, and I was praying. But he got home with a box full of fish. [*laughs*]

WALSH: Oh, Billie, that's wonderful. What is your favorite singing spot? Do you have one of those?

HOLIDAY: Well, no, but, uh—no, no *favorite* singing spot. I'm at Jazz City now and—in fact I was, I closed last night—but I like, mostly places like Carnegie Hall. You know *concerts*, because people really listen to you in those places, you know? Nobody's drinking or smoking, you know—they concentrate, you know? And next to the concerts I like nightclubs, 'cause everybody's happy and having a ball! [*laughs*]

WALSH: But you feel—

HOLIDAY: Theaters I don't care too much about—scares me.

WALSH: Do you feel there's a difference between the audience that you might encounter in Los Angeles, at Jazz City for example, or in New York, or in Honolulu, or—

HOLIDAY: Oh, there's a difference in all this, all over the country.

WALSH: Well, how do you please the audiences all over the country so well, then?

HOLIDAY: Oh, I don't know. [*laughs*]

WALSH: What is the fundamental difference?

HOLIDAY: Well, I don't know. What is that Eddie Cantor or somebody said? "They love me in Boston . . ." [*laughs*] Besides, I really don't know—

WALSH: Well, would you sing—

HOLIDAY: —because people have been nice to me all over, so far.

WALSH: Would you sing different songs in, uh, New York than you would in Los Angeles or Honolulu?

HOLIDAY: [*pauses*] No.

WALSH: You would program the same numbers?

HOLIDAY: Yes, because I go by, uh, my public. They ask me, you know, as a rule, before I go on, they'll ask for like a tune I wrote, "Don't Explain," they'll ask for that. They'll ask for "Strange Fruit," "Sing the Blues Billie," you know . . . so I go by them, I try to please them.

WALSH: Well, one way to certainly please your listeners [*Billie laughs slightly*] is to hear one of your Clef recordings called "Please Don't Talk About Me While I'm Gone," and one that I'm sure warrants many requests when you make an appearance.

[*song plays*]

HOLIDAY [*off air*]: Now are we through?

WALSH: Well, I—

PRODUCER OFF MIC: Uh, just a really quick wrap-up on it, Billie. Why don't you, George, ask her about who's backing her on this song, if you would?

WALSH: All right.

HOLIDAY: Who is—?

MAN OFF MIC: "Please Don't Talk About Me."

HOLIDAY: Oh, my god—

MAN: Uh, wait a minute, uh—

HOLIDAY: Oh, Benny Carter . . .

MAN: Harry Edison.

HOLIDAY: Harry Edison. Um . . .

MAN: Red Callender—

HOLIDAY: Red Callender on bass. Uh, Jimmy, Jimmy—

MAN: Oh no, John Simmons on bass—

HOLIDAY: —John Simmons on bass. Jimmy Rowles on piano. Oh, I can't think of any more. I don't know who's on—

MAN: Is Barney Kessel on—

HOLIDAY: Barney Kessel on guitar.

2ND MAN OFF MIC: Is Jimmy Rowles on piano?

1ST MAN: Uh-huh.

HOLIDAY: And, uh, wait a minute—What did I say? Was six pieces, wasn't it?

MAN: Yeah. You got it—

HOLIDAY: Woah, ah, wait a minute. There was a tenor man. Who was it?

2ND MAN: Is Cozy Cole on drums?

1ST MAN: It was an alto, Billy Carter.

HOLIDAY: Uh, Billy Carter . . .

1ST MAN: Sweets Edison.

HOLIDAY: Sweets Edison, trumpet . . .

1ST MAN: There was no tenor, right?

HOLIDAY: You've got me confused. Benny Carter. Jimmy Rowles, piano, Sweets Edison, trumpet—

1ST MAN: Barney Kessel.

HOLIDAY: Barney Kessel, guitar. Um . . .

1ST MAN: John Simmons, bass.

HOLIDAY: Bass. Where am I, Daddy, it was six pieces.

[*song ends*]

WALSH: Another selection by our special *Green Room* guest, Mademoiselle Billie Holiday, from the Clef album just released called *Velvet Moon*. I understand they're going to release another album of yours in the very near future Billie. I under—

PRODUCER: Let's start over. M-O-O-D. Mood.

WALSH: Oh, *Velvet Mood*! I had moon.

HOLIDAY: Yeah, I tried to tell you before, but you didn't pay me attention.

WALSH: Mmm . . . [*Holiday laughs*] I just thought you were worrying over there. [*they laugh*] Are we rolling Dick? Another selection by our special greenroom guest this afternoon, Mademoiselle Billie Holiday, from the new Clef album, *Velvet Mood*. Billie, I understand they're going to release another album of yours in the near future.

HOLIDAY: Yes, they are, and I have got some swell cats on there with me.

WALSH: Wonderful. Who is backing you up on that?

HOLIDAY: Oh, I have Benny Carter and an alto, and Harry Edison, trumpet, John Simmons, base, and Jimmy Rowles on piano, Barney Kessel. We had a ball.

WALSH: Well, they certainly are some swell cats, as you so aptly put it. I understand, too, that they're going to release a song about your book, carries the same title.

HOLIDAY: Yes. I wrote, um, a little melody called "Lady Sings the Blues."

WALSH: We'll certainly be looking for that. Billy, it certainly has been a pleasure to meet you and to be able to chat with you in person in the greenroom this afternoon. We hope that you'll stop by and see us again real soon.

HOLIDAY: I will and thank you.

VOICE OF AMERICA JAZZ HOUR

INTERVIEW WITH WILLIS CONOVER
MARCH 20, 1956

Editor's Note: The introductory question to this interview was not preserved.

BILLIE HOLIDAY: I think I copied my style from Louis Armstrong, because I always liked, um, the big volume and the big sound that, uh, Bessie Smith got when she sang. But when I was quite young, I heard a record Louis Armstrong made called the "West End Blues," and . . . he doesn't say any words, you know? And I thought, "This is wonderful," you know? And I liked the, the feeling you got from it. So I wanted Louis Armstrong's feeling and I wanted the big volume that Bessie Smith got. But, I found that it didn't work with me because I didn't have a big voice, you know? So, anyway, between the two of 'em, I sorta . . . got Billie Holiday. [*laughs*]

WILLIS CONOVER: Well, what other musicians have had some sort of influence upon the development of your singing style?

HOLIDAY: Well, I, uh, I like Lester Young. I always liked— well, Lester came much later in my life, but I liked Lester's, um, *feeling*, you know? You know, everyone, when he first started, thought, "Man, his tone is too thin," you know? For a tenor sax, you know? Everybody thinks it has to be real big, and Lester used to go out of his mind getting reeds, you know, to sound big like Chu Berry, which was—he was very popular in those days. And I told him it doesn't matter because—I said, "You have a beautiful tone." I said, "And you watch, after a while everybody's going to be copying you." [*laughs*] And it came to be, you know?

And then, well, I made my first record with Benny. Benny came to a club Harlem to hear me, the Log Cabin. At that time, he was not *Benny Goodman*; he was just another musician. [*laughs*] He worked in the studio band, down at NBC, and he came up one night and he just thought I was wonderful. So he had a recording date under his own name, and uh, John Hammond—you must of heard of him, he's a music critic—and uh, they thought I was it, for the vocalist. And the funniest thing, [*laughs*] I got there and I was afraid to sing in the mic, because I never saw a microphone before, and I said, "Why do I have to sing in that thing? Why can't I just sing like I do at the club?" I was scared to death of it. And, uh, Buck and Bubbles,** um, uh, Buck played the piano on that day. Can you imagine? All those studio men and Buck, he can't read a note, he's playing the piano! Well, that's the way Benny is. He likes the music. You don't have to read, or write, or anything. Just play it, you know? So,

---

* Buck and Bubbles was a popular song and dance duo. Buck was Ford Lee "Buck" Washington.

Buck says, "You not gonna let these people think you're a square, are you?" He goes, "Come on, sing it." And I sang, "Your Mother's Son in Law," and on the other side was "Riffin' the Scotch."

CONOVER: So you were fifteen years old then, weren't you?

HOLIDAY: No, I was fourteen.

CONOVER: I beg your pardon.

[*Holiday laughs*]

CONOVER: Well, which of, of your records, Billie, give you more pleasure today? Or perhaps I should rephrase that— what different kinds of pleasure do you get from the earlier recordings and from the more recent records that you've made?

HOLIDAY: Well, I get a big bang out of "Your Mother's Son in Law." It sounds like I'm doing comedy. [*laughs*] My voice sounds so funny and high on there. I sound like I'm about three years old, to me. [*laughs*] And, uh, but the thing that I—I don't like any of my records, to be truthful with you. Because it's always something that you've should've done, or you should've waited here, or you should've held that note longer, or you should've phrased that—you know how it is. So you're never really satisfied with your records.

But the things that I like most, I think the things that don't strain, or the, the ones, the real blues ones, you know? Like, "Summertime." You know? The ones with no music at all, you know, where we just relax. Like the things we did, um, with Teddy Wilson, and Benny, and Roy Eldridge. And we had, uh, I was with Count Basie's band at the time, and we had been on the road about three months, doing one-nighters, you know, and that's pretty rough. And we had no time to rehearse or anything, and we walk right into the studio. No music, and we made six great sides, you know. Those are the kinds I like.

CONOVER: Billie, uh, you recorded so many songs. Which of the songs that you have recorded did you compose yourself?

HOLIDAY: Oh, I uh, I did "Billie's Blues" . . . and "Fine and Mellow" . . . and um . . . Oh, let me tell you how I did "Fine and Mellow." I was working at Café Society, downtown in the Village, and we get in there to make these records, and all of a sudden we need one more side. So I says, "I know, let's do a blues, and let's make the introduction like an organ growl. You know, [*singing*] Da-Da-Da-Da-Ah. You know? And, uh, like that I made it all up right in the studio.

And, I did "Don't Explain" . . . and, hmm what else? [*laughing*] I can't think of . . . But uh, "Don't Explain," I did that with a fellow named Razoff;* he helped me with the lyrics. But, gee, I'm very proud of that because I think it's a pretty tune.

Oh! And I did "God Bless the Child;" don't let me forget

---

*   Holiday seems to be referring here to Andy Razoff, who was the famous lyricist to Fats Waller's "Ain't Misbehaving." The credited coauthor of "Don't Explain," however, is Arthur Herzog, Jr., who was also coauthor of "God Bless the Child."

that one, because I wrote that for my mother. And how it came about, I asked mother for some money, and she flatly refused me. So I says, "That's all right. God bless the child that's got his own." And I walked out, you know? And then it sort of stuck in my mind. And, uh, my piano player and I were fooling around the next day. I says, "You know that's a good title for a song." I said, "But maybe we'll have to make it kind of religious." So he says "No!" So, we—I write out the words, and we get the melody and we wrote the song. So I gave it to Marks,** in publishing? He said it was wonderful and right away he published it. So that's how we got "God Bless the Child."

CONOVER: Are these your favorite records of those you've made Billie?

HOLIDAY: No! [*laughs*] No. Things that I, like I told you, the things that I've made that I like never got popular. Like "Deep Song" . . . you probably never heard of it. [*laughs*] Decca. It never got popular. "You're My Thrill." It is, I think it's got a beautiful background, the strings and the oboe and . . . it never got popular. Like Benny Goodman always says, uh, like the "Some Other Spring" I did. The song "Nothing Ever Happens" is the most beautiful thing I've ever heard in my life. Teddy Wilson, Irene Wilson's, uh, his wife, wrote it. She got inspired; one night we were all playing up there, Benny Webster, and Benny Carter, and myself, and John Kirby the bass player, and we're in her apartment having a jam session there, and she had made some red beans and rice that night. [*laughs*] And

---

*   Edward B. Marks, of Edward B. Marks Music Company.

we were just sitting around playing, and she got inspired and wrote the tune. But like Benny says, "That's not gonna, nothing's gonna happen with that tune. It's too beautiful." And he just didn't make sense to us, you know, but he was right. He says, "Maybe in the years to come." Now, for instance, like "Yesterdays," that's a tune that I recorded and I loved it, but Benny was right, because um,—what was the show? *Roberta*?** It came from *Roberta*, I think. But anyway, uh, "Only Have Eyes for You," that was popular—all the other tunes, "Yesterdays," is the most beautiful song in the show, and it's just starting to get popular now. So, maybe Benny was right! [*laughs*]

CONOVER: What other songs that you haven't recorded would you like to record someday, Billie?

HOLIDAY: Well, I don't know. I'll tell you a song I'd like to sing, and it doesn't have any lyrics to it, I don't think, and that's "Our Waltz," [*pauses*] by David Rose. [*singing*] Da, da, da, da, yaaaa!—

CONOVER: Oh, "Our Waltz," yes.

HOLIDAY: [*laughs*] —You know? Things like that. Something nobody else does.

CONOVER: Well, let's get away from the musical end of Billie Holiday for just a second and ask how the name "Lady Day" came about.

---

* *Roberta* was a 1933 Broadway musical with a score by Jerome Kern and Otto Harbach.

HOLIDAY: Well, now that came about when Lester and I were in Count Basie's band and, um, Lester named me "Lady Day" and he named my mother "Duchess," and there was Count Basie, so we were the royal family. [*laughs*]

CONOVER: I see. Well, then, how did the gardenia in the Billie Holiday hairdo become Billie's trademark?

HOLIDAY: Well, I've always loved gardenias, and one night I, uh, got very, very . . . how would you say it? Well, I guess, I guess, um . . . well, I don't know, there's a word for it. Anyway, I just wouldn't go on, I couldn't go on, I couldn't sing without my gardenia. [*laughs*] So, it became a trademark, and I just thought I couldn't sing if I didn't have a gardenia in my hair, and it had to be fresh. [*laughs*]

CONOVER: You're no longer wearing the gardenia these days, though.

HOLIDAY: Well, no, I got over that. It was just a childish thing. [*laughs*]

CONOVER: "Lady Day." Billie Holiday, our in-person guest today on the *Voice of America Jazz Hour*. Thank you very much, Billie.

HOLIDAY: Thank you, Willis, for having me here.

NIGHT BEAT
(DUMONT TELEVISION)

INTERVIEW WITH MIKE WALLACE
NOVEMBER 8, 1956

Editor's Note: The introductory question to this interview was not preserved.

BILLIE HOLIDAY: Well, I heard a record of, as we call him, Pops,** and it was called "West End Blues," and there was a lady, that um, we would call, she had a little fast house, a sporting house, and I used to run errands for her, and uh, he would say [*singing*] "Oh we da, oh we da we do," and I'd wonder *why* he didn't sing any words, and he had the most beautiful feeling, you know?

MIKE WALLACE: Uh huh.

HOLIDAY: So I wanted his feeling and I wanted Bessie's, uh, big volume. She had a big loud sound. [*laughs*]

WALLACE: And you got 'em both. You know, you talk with such affection about Bessie Smith, Louis Armstrong. There

---

* Louis Armstrong.

seems to be uh, a real companionship, Lady, among the greats in the jazz world. It doesn't seem to be as competitive a field as some others. In some other fields, when you get up there, why, it's kinda cut throat, and in the jazz field, the jazz greats seem to love one another and work with one another.

HOLIDAY: You mean like, when Dizzy,* and Louis, and myself, and Ella, when we all get together?

WALLACE: Yeah, yeah.

HOLIDAY: Well, I guess we all suffered, 'cause we all have it. So, when we get there, we appreciated it.

WALLACE: You appreciate it—

HOLIDAY: That's the only thing I can say.

WALLACE: I imagine that's so . . .

HOLIDAY: That's the way I feel about it.

WALLACE: Were you a good friend of the late Art Tatum, the great jazz pianist who died just a few days ago?

HOLIDAY: Oh, yes . . . He loved my mother so much and Mom loved him, and, whenever he would come to New York or was around, he would stop with us and—I'll tell you a

---

* Dizzy Gillespie.

funny story. Him and Bernie Hanighen—you must of heard of Bernie Hanighen—he wrote songs.

WALLACE: Sure.

HOLIDAY: So, uh, Bernie Hanighen and him got in a little tiff one morning in front of Jimmy's Chicken Shack in Harlem. I don't know if I should tell this story or not, Bernie'll probably shoot me. And uh, Art kept saying, "Bernie leave me alone, leave me alone now, I don't wanna hit ya." And, you know, he couldn't even tell where Bernie was, but I won't talk about his sense of direction. So, Bernie was behind him, so he couldn't kick him in front. So he turns around and he kicked him in the back!

[*they laugh*]

HOLIDAY: Oh, I knew Art very well. He was my dear friend.

WALLACE: Was he a kind man? Was he an expressive man? And was he unhappy?

HOLIDAY: Well, you could tell from his music! [*laughs*]

WALLACE: Yes.

HOLIDAY: He was the end. He was a doll.

WALLACE: Ah, of course, speaking about Art Tatum, do you have any idea how old he was when he died?

HOLIDAY: I don't know, but I don't think Art could've been more than about fifty-six, fifty-four years old, something like that.

WALLACE: Oh, was he, was he that old?

HOLIDAY: He was in his fifties, yeah. I'm sure he was.

WALLACE: Because the question, uh, the question, Billie, that I was going to ask was that why so many jazz greats seem to die so early? Now, uh, Bix Beiderbecke it happened to, Fats Waller wasn't too old, Charlie Parker, Frankie Tesche-macher . . .

HOLIDAY: Well, Mike, the only way I can answer that question is, we try to live one hundred days in one day and we try to please so many people, and we try to—like myself, I wanna bend this note and bend that note, and sing this way and sing that way, and get all the feeling and eat all the good foods and travel all in one day, and you can't do it. [*laughs*] So I think that's why.

WALLACE: Of course, there's one spot in your book in partic-ular that I think revealed a little bit of you and it didn't seem to me that you liked, perhaps, to live that way that much anymore. I'd like to quote back something that you wrote in your book. It was a line that had a good deal of meaning and simplicity. You wrote as follows, Lady: "You've got to have something to eat and a little love in your life. Everything I am and everything I want out of life goes smack back to that." Now, when did you discover that, and what does that mean to you, Billie?

HOLIDAY: Well, we all have to eat and we all have to sleep, and I . . . was hungry so long! [*laughs*]

WALLACE: Mmm hmm . . .

HOLIDAY: —And, now that I do know how to eat, and sleep, and I have travelled . . . Ask me that question again. I can answer it better than that.

WALLACE: All right, let's—actually as you started to, as I read it, and as you started to answer, I discovered that what you said a little earlier was right. You like to, you like to take life by the forelock and live it while you've got it, and that's why, as you suggested, some jazz performers die young because they *do*. They get a little to eat and a little to love and—

HOLIDAY: Yeah, and when you get it you use it, you know . . . [*laughs*]

WALLACE: You use it.

HOLIDAY: Yeah— [*laughs*]

WALLACE: Life is to use, is the way that you feel. But again, I'll give it to you. You gotta have something to eat and a little love in your life.

HOLIDAY: You must have love—

WALLACE: Mmm hmm . . .

HOLIDAY: —You see, all I had was my mom. I never had brothers or sisters, or cousins, or uncles, or people running in and out. All we had was one preacher and he used to come every Sunday. And mama said, "Oh, go on, eat all you like Revered so-and-so—" I can't even think of his name. And myself, in those days, I did have a cousin; I had a cousin Charlie and a cousin Dorothy. And that day the children had to wait. And he would eat, and he'd bring his wife and his whole family sometimes. And we'd wait and we'd wind up with the *gravy*. So, one Sunday, I just made a boo-boo, and I says, "Mama, you know there's no more in the pot!"

[*they laugh*]

So what do I do? I got a whipping.

[*they laugh*]

WALLACE: Um, you've mentioned some of your good friends who are musicians, Billie. But, I know a couple of good friends of yours who are not musicians and I'd like to know how you got to know them, and what it is that you have most in common with them. There are two names in particular. Well, I, no, I'll give you three: Tallulah Bankhead, and Charles Laughton, and Orson Welles.

HOLIDAY: Well, I . . . I think I knew them, well, I don't think, I know I knew them because, well, they was just brave enough to come up to Harlem when they was starting Jazz.

[*they laugh*]

At that time, you know, most people were afraid to come to Harlem, and those that did, um, you know, it was one of those things—[*singing*] it was just one of those things—but anyway . . . [*laughs*]

WALLACE: How long ago was that?

HOLIDAY: Uh oh. Now don't go tellin' my age now.

[*they laugh*]

Well, I was, uh, just starting; I was only about fourteen, and I'll never forget the night I met Mr. Laughton. He came in and I had no idea he was a movie actor. And he was looking for his valet, that's how he got wandering around up there. [*laughs*]

WALLACE: Up in Harlem?

HOLIDAY: [*laughs*] Yeah. And, uh, I think his name was George, and he was just looking for George, and uh, George had told him about me.

WALLACE: Yeah.

HOLIDAY: And he's asking for Billie Holiday, he's looking for George, and I said, "Who's that man? Who's asking for me?" That's how we got acquainted. And, um, afterwards he always comes to hear me sing whenever he's around. He's been very kind. Uh, Ms. Bankhead, I think she's the end. I love her. In fact, I think it's, uh, three ladies: Miss Barrymore, Miss Bankhead, and uh, you know Helen.*

WALLACE: Well, now, when you mention people like Ethel Barrymore or Tallulah Bankhead—is it the fact that you are performers, the three of you? Is that what you have in common? Or do you feel that they've been—

HOLIDAY: They're not performers, they are, uh, actresses, actors! I look at them like—whoo! [*laughs*]

WALLACE: And you don't consider yourself in the same league?

HOLIDAY: No! My god, no! [*laughs*]

WALLACE: Why not? Now, why not? You've worked as hard.

* Actor Helen Hayes.

You've thought as much about it. You have developed a style, a technique, just as much as they have done. You please just as many people. So what're you worried—why don't you feel that you have the same quality? Why are you not just as much an artiste as any one of them?

HOLIDAY: Well, maybe I am in my little way, but, my god, they . . . they make me cry. They make me happy. I don't know if I've ever done that to people, not really.

WALLACE: Oh, I think you do.

[*Billie laughs*]

I think you do know that.

HOLIDAY: Maybe I do . . .

WALLACE: You know, one of the most remarkable things about jazz performers is that, white or colored, you're way ahead of so many of the rest of us when it comes to desegregation. I heard a story about you this afternoon, as a matter of fact, from a good friend of yours by the name of Leonard Feather.

HOLIDAY: Wow. He is my boy. I love Leonard.

WALLACE: And Leonard told me about the time, Leonard and Bob Bach, told me about the time, when, um, you sang at The Ritz, in Boston, at The Ritz Carlton, in Boston, and there was still a policy—

HOLIDAY: Wow, up on the roof!

WALLACE: That's right!

HOLIDAY: [*laughs raucously*] Yeah!

WALLACE: And there was still a policy of, uh, of no colored singers being with a white organization. Would you tell that story to us now, about you and Helen Forrest?

HOLIDAY: Well, that, uh, I-I-I'd rather not. I mean, it was a drag. It was a drag for Helen, too, because she was a sweet kid, and they said I couldn't sit on the bandstand, which I didn't want to do; I never did. I never—

WALLACE: They said in Boston that you couldn't sit on the bandstand?

HOLIDAY: Well, they didn't want to, uh, they—Artie** had a rule that we both should sit on the bandstand, you know. In fact, Tony Pastor,†** you know, he was, uh, blowin' in the band, he played tenor. So, I says, "It's all right for Tony, he's got something to do."

WALLACE: Mmm hmm . . .

HOLIDAY: I said, "I feel like a fool sitting up here." Just sittin', you know, waitin' ten, fifteen, twenty minutes before I sang—

---

*   Bandleader Artie Shaw.
†   Tony Pastor was both a singer and tenor saxophone player.

WALLACE: Right.

HOLIDAY: —I says, "And Artie, I don't like it."

WALLACE: Mmm hmm . . .

HOLIDAY: So whenever, I—you know, when it was all right, I would sneak off, I'd have business in the ladies' room or somewhere [*laughs*], but poor Helen, she'd have to sit there. So when we finally got to The Ritz Carlton that was a big, good deal for me, because I didn't have to sit. You know?

WALLACE: Yeah.

HOLIDAY: So anyway, Helen and I both, you know, uh, oh she was sweet about the whole deal. She was a wonderful girl about that.

WALLACE: Mmm hmm . . .

HOLIDAY: She says, "I don't see why, ah, if I can sit here why Lady can't sit." You know?

WALLACE: Yeah.

HOLIDAY: So I said, "I don't want to sit. Do you remember us?" [*laughs*] So, it was one of those things. But, anyway— well, it worked out very nicely.

WALLACE: Mmm hmm . . . Well, why is it that the color

thing has not ever really been that important with musicians as it is with some of the rest of us in the USA.

HOLIDAY: Well, I think, the only answer I can give to that is, I guess we have more nerve than other people. And, uh, we get a chance to meet more people, and bigger people. Like, we get a chance, like I met Roosevelt's son. How did I meet him? In Café Society.**

WALLACE: Mmm hmm . . .

HOLIDAY: You know, and I had nerve enough to go over and say, "Hello, aren't you Roosevelt's son?" And he's not gonna say, "Get away from my table." You know, he's gonna say, "Hello, who are you?" You know?

WALLACE: Mmm hmm . . .

HOLIDAY: So I think we have uh, more of an opportunity to meet people. And if they are real people, you know, nice people, they ain't gonna shove us around, you know?

WALLACE: Mmm hmm . . .

HOLIDAY: So I think that's why, uh, musicians, and actors, and artists, can, uh, sort of straighten all that deal out. [*laughs*] That's the way I can put it.

---

*   One of Manhattan's leading nightclubs, which was located in Greenwich Village.

WALLACE: And because talent, ah, it's been said –

HOLIDAY: And if you get up and sing or dance, or make a speech, and if you have nerve enough to give them all a show, and they like it . . .

WALLACE: Yeah.

HOLIDAY: You know?

WALLACE: And all . . .

HOLIDAY: So everybody gets to be one happy family—

WALLACE: And all things are equal.

HOLIDAY: —[*laughs*] that's the only way I can explain it.

WALLACE: I understand, I know, that one of the reasons for your present happiness is your husband, Louis. Now you say that—in your book—that he was a preacher when he was fifteen years old?

HOLIDAY: He certainly was. You should hear his mother, she's eighteen years old, her—eighty-nine years old. Eighteen! Whoo, wow, I hope she's not listening to this program. [*Wallace laughs*] She's eighty-nine years old, and uh, Louis had a dog, and he loved this dog so much, and she said the dog, he was terrible, his hair was all over the place, there were fleas, and this and that. Anyway, the dog died, and Louis buried the dog, and he preached it. And, years later, when we got married, we go to Buffalo, we're walking down the street, and somebody says, "Hey Preach, come here man."

[*Wallace laughs*]

Well, I kept right on going, and he just sort of turns around, "Hey Preach, what's the matter? You don't know me no more now? Hey Preach!" So I says, "What's wrong with that man?" He says, "He's calling me." [*laughs*] That's how I found out the story, why all his hometown people call him "Preach."

WALLACE: Well, as a former preacher, how does he react to some of your more torrid blues songs? Some of the more suggestive lyrics?

HOLIDAY: Oh now, he tells me how to sing, and what to sing, and oh, it's just getting terrible. [laughs] He can't even tap his foot.

[*they laugh*]

WALLACE: Tell me this, what, what, what is it that you want out of life professionally? As a matter of fact, if we can, if we can ask you a thing like this, and ask for a quick answer: What is it that you're after out of life yourself, Billie, now?

HOLIDAY: Right now?

WALLACE: Yeah.

HOLIDAY: I want a beautiful home, and I want kids, and I like to cook. And if you ever come to my house—have you ever had, you ever had any southern cookin'?

WALLACE: Oh, indeed I have.

HOLIDAY: I bet you've never eaten pig's feet.

WALLACE: Any pig's feet?

HOLIDAY: Yeah.

WALLACE: Oh sure, I've had pigs feet.

HOLIDAY: Chitlins?

WALLACE: Chitlins too. There's a girl—

HOLIDAY: Greens? [*laughs*]

WALLACE: —there's a girl who works for me, there's a girl who works for me out in the country. Her name is Anne Cheek.

HOLIDAY: Yeah?

WALLACE: And she can cook up a storm, believe me.

HOLIDAY: Well, that's the kind of stuff I like to cook.

WALLACE: In addition to which, I'm married to a girl who lived down in Haiti for a long time.

HOLIDAY: Wow.

WALLACE: And she likes rice and beans. And I understand that rice and beans is one of your favorite dishes.

HOLIDAY: Red beans!

WALLACE: Yeah.

HOLIDAY: Red beans. Right, I take, uh, I got, uh, uh, a nice top of the round steak and I have it ground up, ya' know?

WALLACE: Yeah.

HOLIDAY: And I put garlic, and green peppers, and onions and, oh wow, and the beans, you know, and I boil them down. And I make my pig's feet, after I boil them, I bake them and I bake them until they're almost like potato chips.

WALLACE: As crisp as that?

HOLIDAY: That's right.

WALLACE: Mmm hmm. But what you want out of life then is a home and kids . . . ?

HOLIDAY: That's right. And I want to be able to have my own club. I want a small club.

WALLACE: A club, you mean, in which you'll uh—

HOLIDAY: My own club—

WALLACE: —sing and cook, too? [*laughs*]

HOLIDAY: —I'm working. If I feel like singing eighty-nine songs, I can. If I want to sing two songs, I can. If I don't feel like going to work, I don't have to. I want a little place, a hole, maybe 150–200 people. Very cozy, you know? Just all my friends, and . . . everybody else who wants to come.

WALLACE: Why, sure.

HOLIDAY: That's what I want.

WALLACE: And I think that probably everybody who comes is bound to be a friend of yours, Billie.

HOLIDAY: Thank you.

WALLACE: Billie, thank you for coming and letting us learn a little bit about you here on *Night Beat*, tonight.

HOLIDAY: It's been wonderful talking to you.

WALLACE: We're going to, uh, come see you Saturday night—

HOLIDAY: Thank you.

WALLACE: —in concert, at Carnegie Hall.

HOLIDAY: Thank you very much.

WALLACE: Billie Holiday, who's become a legend in her own time, partially because she's been knocked around a good deal, and because the world knows about it. But, there's a more important reason, too. Billie, Lady, is a legend because she's a great singer, and a courageous human being.

STATEMENT OF MRS. ELANOR GOUGH MCKAY, ALSO KNOWN AS MISS BILLIE HOLIDAY

TAKEN IN THE OFFICE OF THE SUPERVISING CUSTOM AGENT, 201 VARICK STREET, NEW YORK 14, N.Y., ROOM 455 3:40 P.M. ON JANUARY 15, 1959.

PRESENT:

    MRS. ELANOR GOUGH McKAY
       (Miss BILLIE HOLIDAY) ————DEPONENT

    [REDACTED]————————————Customs Agent

    [REDACTED]————————————Customs Agent

    Miss Florynce R. Kennedy,
      6 East 46th Street,
      New York 17, N.Y. ———— Deponent's Attorney

    [REDACTED] ———— Shorthand Reporter.

(BY [REDACTED])

Q. Mrs. McKay, Agent [REDACTED] and I are customs agents of the United States Treasury Department. You are here at our invitation in connection with an investigation we are conducting relative to your having departed from and reentered the United States without having registered in accordance with the narcotic registration law, about which we desire to ask you certain questions. Are you willing to answer our questions?

A. Yes.

Q. I want to advise you that under the Constitution of the United States you are not compelled to answer any questions, but if you do, and the Government desires, they may use your answers against you. Is this clear, and in the circumstances are you willing to answer our questions truthfully?

A. Yes.

Q. Will you stand and raise your right hand, please? Do you solemnly swear that the statements you are about to make will be the truth, the whole truth and nothing but the truth, so help you God?

A. (Standing and with raised right hand) I do.

Q. What is your name, age and occupation?

A. My name is BILLIE HOLIDAY. I am forty-one. I am a singer; that's my occupation.

Q. Is your true name MRS. ELEANOR GOUGH McKAY?*

A. Yes.

---

* Note that Customs transcribers recorded Holiday's actual first name in two different spellings in this document. However, neither is correct. On her birth certificate, Holiday's first name was reportedly spelled 'Elinore,' but throughout her life she preferred the spelling 'Eleanora.'

Q. The name of Billie Holiday is your—

A. Stage name.

Q. —professional or stage name?

A. Yes.

Q. Where do you live?

A. 26 West 37th Street.

Q. Apartment?

A. 1-B

(BY [REDACTED])

Q. Are you a citizen of the United States, Miss Holiday?

A. Yes.

Q. I show your passport no. 1047225. Was this issued to you for travel abroad by the United States Department of State?

A. It was, yes.

(BY [REDACTED])

Q. At this time, Mrs. McKay, in the event you don't fully understand any of our questions, will you please refer to your attorney, Miss Kennedy, before you answer, if you so desire? Where were you born?

A. Baltimore, Maryland.

Q. Did you say Baltimore, Maryland? Your passport lists Philadelphia, Pennsylvania, as the place of your birth on April 7, 1915. What is the correct—?

A. I went to school in Baltimore. I always say Baltimore. I went to school in Baltimore. It's a mistake. I'm sorry.

Q. Then you want to correct that answer?

A. Yes, that's right.

Q. Were you born in Philadelphia, Pennsylvania, on April 7, 1915?

A. April 7, 1915.

Q. That would make you forty-three years of age now.

(BY [REDACTED])

Q. Did you leave the United States about the end of October 1956?

A. Yes I did

Q. Where did you travel to?

A. We went to Paris, we stayed there one day and then we went to Milano, Italy.

(BY [REDACTED])

Q. Where did you leave the United States from?

A. New York.

Q. Was that from Idlewild Airport in Queens County?

A. Yes.

(BY [REDACTED])

Q. When did you return to the United States? Approximately, if you don't remember the exact date?

A. (Referring to passport) The 2nd of December.

(BY [REDACTED])

Q. Was that at Idlewild Airport in Queens County?

A. No, we didn't. We come back to LaGuardia. Yes, I remember distinctly.

Q. Was that due to a weather condition?

A. Yes.

(BY [REDACTED])

Q. Have you ever been convicted of any narcotic offences—

A. Yes, I have.

Q. —of the Federal Government or any state thereof?

A. The Federal Government, once. I was sent to Alderson, West Virginia; did one year.

Q. Were you convicted or did you plead guilty? What were the circumstances?

A. I wanted to go away for a cure, and they gave me—

Q. I have a copy of your record from the Federal Bureau of Investigation, which indicates that on May 26th, 1947, as Billie Holiday, you received a sentence of one year and one day at the Federal Reformatory for Women at Alderson, West Virginia. Is this a true record?

A. Yes, that's right.

(BY [REDACTED])

Q. Was this sentence that Mr. [REDACTED] just mentioned as a result of a conviction in the United States Court House in the Southern District of New York at Foley Square?

A. No, that was in Philadelphia.

Q. You were arrested at Philadelphia by Federal narcotic agents?

A. No, I wasn't really arrested. They were sort of like you people; they were very nice to me.

Q. You were brought to court and then you pleaded guilty?

A. Yes.

(OFF THE RECORD)

(BY [REDACTED])

Q. Mrs. McKay, from your acknowledged prior narcotic conviction, you apparently fall into the category of persons required to register as narcotic convictees in accordance with the narcotic registration law. Are you familiar with that?

A. No, I am not.

Q. Did you know of the law requiring persons to register as a narcotic convictee on leaving and reentering the United States?

A. No, I did not, sir.

(BY [REDACTED])

Q. This law also applies to persons who are users of narcotics as well.

A. I didn't know anything about it at all.

Q. When you left the United States on this trip to France and Italy, did you have in your possession any narcotics for your own personal use?

A. No, sir.

Q. Were you a user of narcotics at the time you left the United States?

A. No, sir.

Q. What was the purpose in leaving the United States.

A. I went there to sing, to do concerts.

Q. You went for a professional engagement abroad?

A. That's right. Just myself and my piano player. And my agent gave me the tickets, he gets the tickets and gives us the airplane tickets and tells us where to go and who to meet, and he never tells us about registering. I never saw any sign, so I didn't know. I went to the doctor, I did everything else I should have done, so why shouldn't I have done this? I did not know.

Q. Who is your piano player?

A. His name is Mal Waldron.

Q. Does he leave the United States and return to the United States with you?

A. Yes.

(BY [REDACTED])

Q. Where does he live?

A. He lives in St. Albans, Long Island. I have his address some place. (Consults small address books without success)

Q. He's listed in the phone book?

(BY MISS KENNEDY)

A. He is in the phone book and it's under St. Albans. His father is also listed.

Q. What would his full name be?

(BY MISS HOLIDAY)

A. Malcolm.

(BY [REDACTED])

Q. Did you register when you left the United States and when you returned, as a convicted narcotic violator, with customs?

A. No. Nobody asked me to, I never did it before. This must be something new, because wouldn't they ask me?

Q. No. It's not the Government's responsibility to ask every individual passenger or person leaving the United States if they have a narcotic record.

A. Or coming back?

Q. No, because you'd be insulting a lot of people.

A. Oh, yes, I suppose so . . . I really didn't know it, and I didn't see any signs, and I'm awfully sorry about it.

(BY [REDACTED])

Q. I personally want to call your attention to this notice (exhibiting sign), a placard which is posted at the various airports and piers. This is a warning to narcotic users and violators concerning their requirements of registering upon leaving and reentering the United States. Have you ever seen any similar sign before this?

A. No. If I had, I would have noticed it and I would have asked Joe about it, and I would have went and done something about it. Really I don't know anything about it.

(BY [REDACTED])

Q. When you mention "Joe"—?

A. I mean my agent, Mr. Glaser.

Q. Joseph Glaser?

A. Yes. Associated Booking Corporation, 745 Fifth Avenue. No, I didn't know anything about this.

Q. It's clear that you left the United States on a Pan American plane.

A. Yes.

(BY [REDACTED])

Q. And you returned, as I understand, on an Air France plane, is that correct?

A. Yes.

Q. Flight 041 on December 2, 1958.

A. They kept me out there in the cold for half an hour, taking pictures.

Q. Mrs. McKay, have you ever been arrested for narcotic violations other than in May 1947?

A. Yes.

Q. When, please?

A. Oh, about a year ago. But it was all wrong, and it was nothing—

Q. About a year ago?

A. Yes, about a year ago, I think it was. You must have it there.

Q. Where?

A. Philadelphia. There wasn't anything to it, it was all wrong.

Q. Would that have been an arrest on or about February 23, 1956 in Philadelphia, Pennsylvania, by their police department, for narcotic drugs?

A. I think it was the city. Something like that. There was nothing to it.

Q. What was the disposition of the matter?

A. I really don't know. I just went off to work—

(BY MISS KENNEDY)

A. [illegible] what finally happened?

(BY DEPONENT:)

A. Nothing.

Q. You were acquitted, in other words?

A. Yes.

Q. Was there a trial held at which you were found not guilty and acquitted?

A. Yes. Well, you know, they have to trade awhile and pick on you a little bit.

Q. Was there any other time you were arrested for any other narcotic violation?

A. Not that I remember.

Q. Where you arrested in San Francisco—

A. Oh, yes, that was before—

Q. —on or about January 22, 1949?

A. —with John Levy, yes.

Q. And the record shows that that charge was dismissed—

A. That's right.

Q. —on March 2, 1949, is that correct?

A. That's right.

(BY [REDACTED])

Q. You have answered all our questions of your own free will and accord, is that true?

A. Yes.

Q. No threats or promises or any type have been made to you for answering our questions?

A. No, sir.

Q. You have had the advice of your counsel all through this statement?

A. Yes, sir.

(BY [REDACTED)

Q. Is there anything you would like to add to this statement?

A. Yes . . . there's a lot I would like to add, but it would take a book. I'd have to write a book.

Q. Any comments or statements you would like to make you may insert in the record at this time.

A. Well, it just seems that a little thing like this I didn't know about, and nobody cared enough about me—my agents, and I got managers for this and that—to tell me about it, and I have been trying my best to be a good girl, and a little thing like this, I have to come down here and go through all this. That's all I can say. It's terrible that's all. Once you get in trouble for narcotics, it's the end. I think it's the worst thing that could ever happen to anybody in the wide world. That's all I got to add.

(TO DEPONENT'S ATTORNEY)

Q. Miss Kennedy, as attorney for Mrs. McKay, do you have anything to add to this statement?

A. I don't think so, but I hope we make it entirely clear that Miss Holiday's intention has been at all times to comply with whatever rules and regulations there are, and apparently her agent—inasmuch as this law was enacted rather recently, 1956, it had not come to her attention. I realize this is not an excuse, but it's a simple fact that this intelligence had not come to her attention. Apparently her attorney did not know of it.

I, personally—although we were not representing her at this time, we were not aware of it, and had we been representing her we would not have brought it to her attention either because we did not know about it. And I can only say it's a clear case of not being responsible to a law which she had not already become acquainted with; that's about all I can say.

I would just like to make the further request that, if possible, we terminate this as quickly as possible, because I think it can be seen that it has been Miss Holiday's intention to abide by the law.

Q. I am going to refer this matter, with all these statements, to the United States Attorney for the Eastern District of New York at Brooklyn, and I necessarily will be guided by his decision in the matter.

A. Of course.

Q. I will provide him with a copy of the statement, but I would like some arrangements made at this time for the statement to be reviewed by you and Mrs. McKay.

A. Would it be possible for you to provide us with a copy of the statement?

(BY [REDACTED])

Yes.

I have read this statement consisting of 8 pages, have initialed or signed each page, and have made and initiated all necessary corrections. The contents of this statement are true and correct to the best of my knowledge and belief.

_____

Subscribed and sworn to before me this ___ day of _____, 1959.

_____

Customs Agent

Designated to administer oaths, Customs Delegation Order No. 2, T.D. 53195.

_____

Witness.

Transcribed by me from original notes on January 16, 1959.

[REDACTED]

Shorthand Reporter.

THE LAST INTERVIEW: "I NEEDED HEROIN TO LIVE"

BY BILLIE HOLIDAY
CONFIDENTIAL MAGAZINE
OCTOBER 1959

As the following article was written, Billie Holiday, the Lady Day of jazz, lay critically ill in New York's Metropolitan Hospital. During her illness there, a nurse said she detected flecks of heroin on Miss Holiday's face. The singer was placed under arrest on a narcotics charge and, in spite of the fact that her weakness made it obvious she could not escape, a policewoman was stationed in her room. Two days after the article was written, Billie Holiday died.

What follows is her own story of her experiences with heroin, the most powerful of narcotics. The editors of CONFIDENTIAL bring you this story, not because we agree with all of Miss Holiday's views on narcotics—we do not—but because we believe this is a profoundly moving story. We do believe with Miss Holiday that the narcotics addict is entitled to human kindness and to medical treatment administered with the same warmth and decency that any other sick person has the right to expect.

Lying on this hospital bed, knowing that the policewoman's in the room, I keep staring at the big black headlines. "Billie Doomed!" they say. I have to sigh. The policewoman asks, "You feeling sad, Lady Day?" I sigh again and shrug. "We're *all* doomed, baby. You, and me, and *everyone*, we're all doomed!"

It seems the only time I ever make the headlines is when I'm low in soul and have to find a way of getting happy. "Billie Holiday is dying of dope addiction and alcoholism." Nobody wants to read about the times when I felt free and young and crammed with hope and opened up my heart to let the world in.

They forget the laughter and the weeping I brought to people who waited for a voice to sing the happy and the crying songs they wanted so much to hear. They don't remember the woman—they just remember the wreck. That's how people are—they remember someone else's misery to forget their own.

"Her voice is shot—cracked and eroded by the careless years of drug addiction, whiskey drinking and other malign influences . . ."

I never had much voice to begin with, but I've got more today than I ever had.

Just for kicks and because I'm feeling low, I arch my back and sing the first bars of "Night and Day." My tremolo is like a shiver and the feeling is heartache and the policewoman smiles a loving smile and we look into each other's eyes and we know that a judge and jury would back me in a libel suit against anyone who slammed my voice.

Your voice and love for singing hold on tight. It's the sense of hope that leaves you first.

I read aloud: "Whiskey and heroin have taken their toll," says another press report. "The famed jazz singer lies on the verge of death at 44 . . ." and anger is a rip inside me. I crush the paper and tell the policewoman, "My mother and father never touched dope in their lives—and neither of them lived to be as old as me. I've been on and off heroin for fifteen years. So who knows? MAYBE I NEEDED HEROIN TO LIVE!"

The policewoman silently turns away. I know she cries for me; there are some feelings that can't talk.

When I was feeling down on the outside and all alone and all the parts of me were losing pulse, heroin was like a special gland working and filling me with life. Deep in me—where the clear sweet voice of truth sings only to me—I believe it is true that heroin kept me alive.

There's a "meaning" in me that I've never really understood—a "meaning" that has bugged the hospital psychiatrists and other people, too. Maybe it came up to me from my great grandfather, Charles Fagan, an Irish-Catholic, and my great grandmother who was a slave on his Virginia plantation. Part of me is a wild Irish spirit and part of me is the deep brown, earthy beauty of my great grandmother. The combination mixed in me and gave me a "meaning" that made me driving sometimes and sometimes deadly—sometimes sentimental and sometimes riotous and free and other times just soft and bluesy—but way inside of me I know that "meaning" is what makes me want to keep alive, no matter what!

I've been and done a lot of things in my life but all through whatever I've been or done, I've always been a woman. I never felt inferior to anyone and I wouldn't learn to knuckle down and act like I was lower—even if it meant getting the break I always wanted. I never got past the fifth grade in school and maybe that was lucky. I wasn't spoiled by "learning" that might have made me believe that I was less and others were more. The only thing I knew was that I wanted to be more than what I was when I started out. I wanted to stretch high and wide and handsome until I was all of me, Billie Holiday.

But when you're poor and black, you're born into a world that turns your heart into a tin can and anyone who is in the mood swings out and kicks you. You're only a hunk, a black creature in a white world that thinks you're just a skin without a soul. And when the "meaning" in you screams for you to make your stand, you make your stand straight and strong. Then the kicks come faster and harder and you're booted out of shape. But you hold onto your stand, and sometimes it holds you high and sometimes it drags you low—but that's the way it goes. You're a nothing and a nobody if what you believe is only make-believe.

A psychiatrist once asked me why I started taking heroin and all I could tell him was the words of why—but I knew he couldn't *feel* the feelings why. A special "need" starts in you after you've spent all night locked in a room with a dead girl. Waking up one time and finding myself held in the death grip of my great grandmother; held so hard and tight the neighbors had to break my great grandmother's stiff arms to free me. Working in a "house" at thirteen and being beaten and cursed and used as some "good-luck" time by a white man. Knowing that my father died of pneumonia because a Dallas hospital wouldn't admit a Negro. You don't decide to become a junkie. Life sometimes drives you to heroin.

Maybe my life would have been different if during those lazy, crazy, juiced-up, jazzed-up Thirties there had been some psychiatrists who were right and good and interested in helping me. Maybe they would have fed tranquilizing pills to ease the humiliations and heartaches and have guided me around the traps and sewers laid out for a woman whose beauty is dressed in the wrong color. But tranquilizers came out too many years too late.

I used the only tranquilizer I could find—heroin—the happy dust, the stuff that deals out dreams from the lowest kind of deck. And one dream makes you hungry for another dream and the next dream is a better dream and soon you're so hungry for those dreams you have to feed your hunger or you'll die.

"Illegal hunger" they call it. Maybe so. But so were the hungers in the nerves of the people who filled the brothels in which I worked—so were the boozy hungers in the people who came into the joints where I sang. But the Legals winked at their hungers and flashed badges at mine. And it's not too much different now.

The tranquilizers they push today can turn out to be habit-forming and maybe hook people on a deeper hunger. You can buy tranquilizers today, the same way you could get morphine and heroin before 1914—by handing a druggist a doctor's prescription. The label on the bottle usually says, "Habit-Forming. Use only under doctor's supervision." But what DOESN'T the label tell you? The same information the pusher or your "connection doesn't tell you when you pick up a fix. You don't become a drug addict because you use junk. IT'S THE REASON WHY YOU NEED THE DRUGS THAT MAKES AND KEEPS YOU A DRUG ADDICT!

The Legals dump you in a cell and make you "kick" the

habit—but who cares enough to help you kick the "cause?" And, for me, heroin was sometimes the difference between living and dying.

Sometimes a woman has to leave the real world for awhile. She has to drift off to a soft place, or loll in some sweet shadow where she can forget what the terror of being "almost" raped at ten feels like. Forget what her rage against injustice has made her do. Forget about having bashed someone's head with a baseball bat and shoving a girl down a long flight of stairs and jamming another girl's head into a toilet bowl intending to drown her. Sometimes you've got to forget all the gores and wounds the world cuts into you to make you feel you're just a clod of black dirt not worth a kindness or a kiss. Heroin not only kept me alive—maybe it also kept me from killing.

Many's the time I've secretly laughed at those anemic-brained psychiatrists who have branded me "self-destructive," a woman with a "death-wish"—a woman who deliberately puts herself into "killing" situations and whose only end is to be laid on a slab with a tag on her toe marked "suicide." They never really knew me. They were trying to fit a snap lyric onto a long, dreamy melody. I never once thought to "suicide" myself out of this world. I spent my life trying to find a way into this world. And sometimes the only way I really could was when heroin opened the door.

That song I used to sing, "Ain't Nobody's Business What I Do," was more than just a song to me. It was the anthem of my way of life. I always avoided talk about narcotics because narcotics is a medical and social problem. Let the doctors and the teachers sit around and do the discussing. What I did was just nobody's business but my own.

But my arrests—one acquittal, one suspended sentence and one jail term—made my habit the public's business. People almost forgot that I was a jazz singer. When my name came out in print, my police record always seemed to be hanging around. It kept grinding me down and dragging after me and no matter where I went or how hard I tried to lose it, it hung on. So I had to make my stand again and sing out—and no matter how the notes sounded, I wanted people to hear my voice. My book, *Lady Sings the Blues*, sold over two million copies and was translated into fifteen languages, including Japanese.

My "no-holds-barred" way of telling my heart out in story form was treated with a human warmth I had never known before. My comments on the narcotics problem were reprinted in a U.S. medical journal and I was singing, happy because not only had I contributed to the score of human understanding, but for the first time in my life I felt I "belonged."

I proved that the "professional" people in the country know nothing about the "human" side of the drug addict and don't really give a damn about the problem. If they did, they would have found me, and others like me, and have helped us—instead of leaving us to the cops who think that when they pick up some "users" they're cleaning up some garbage from the streets.

THE ONLY ONE WHO REALLY UNDERSTANDS A DRUG ADDICT IS ANOTHER DRUG ADDICT.

How can the doctors know about the "meanings" in a drug addict when they're not allowed to treat us? What can a doctor know about our insides; the way life knots and strangles our feelings and how we wail and scream with tongueless voices, begging for help and knowing, even in our most desperate and tortured hours, that the help we need isn't there? Not even the psychiatrists can help. They're like arm-less piano players pecking out a tune with their toes. As for the cops, they just don't give a damn!

I've been punished to the limit the law allows. I've been man-handled when arrested, jailed and bailed, paroled and jailed again—humiliated, maligned, laughed at, degraded and deprived of income by not being allowed to work in any New York night club where liquor is sold. (Is there any night club in New York that makes its money selling lemonade?) I've been hounded for over twelve years. Is this the way the authorities work to help a person who wants to give herself up for help?

To get help I had to go to Europe where a drug addict isn't treated like a scar on the face of society, but like a human being trying to get off the wrong road. All my own country ever did for me was dump me into an over-crowded jail. If I lived, they'd feed me—and if I died, they'd bury me.

They're watching me now—watching me the way a hawk watches a crippled sparrow. They've taken away my maga-zines and phonograph, my records and my radio. The only thing they let my friends bring me is a jar of yoghurt or a pint of ice cream.

Right here I'm under arrest again—again on a narcotics charge. What they'll eventually do with me, I don't know.

I hold no regrets and I carry no shame. Nobody can laugh or cry for you—you have to laugh or cry all alone. If my life was wrong or right—good or bad—it's still my life and what's about to happen—will happen just to me.

We're all the same, but we're different. What sings in you, sings different in me. It's all part of that great crazy game called living.

But when I leave this lump they call the world, I'm going to leave all my blues behind and walk off singing.

BILLIE HOLIDAY (1915–1959) is widely considered the greatest singer in twentieth century jazz, whose heartfelt phrasing and improvisational skills had a seminal influence on the form. Born in Philadelphia and raised in Baltimore, she emerged from a troubled childhood to quick popularity in Harlem and Manhattan nightclubs, stints in the bands of Artie Shaw and Count Basie, and rising commercial recording success. However, a narcotics bust landed her in prison in 1948, costing her her cabaret license—without which she couldn't perform in New York City nightclubs. This blow compounded problems with her finances, her health, and, devastatingly, her voice. Despite a few triumphant comeback performances at Carnegie Hall and some mildly successful recordings, she never fully recovered her standing, and she died of cirrhosis of the liver in 1959 in a New York hospital—with police stationed at her door, waiting to arrest her on another drug bust should she recover. Holiday was the recipient of four Grammy awards—all of them posthumous.

KHANYA MTSHALI is a journalist and critic from Johannesburg, South Africa. She writes about history, fashion, culture, gender, race, and literature. Her work has been featured in *The Guardian*, *The Mail and Guardian*, *The LA Review of Books*, *Popula*, *The Outline*, *The Rumpus*, and Bookforum.com.

DAVE DEXTER, JR. was an American music journalist who went on to become a record company executive at Capitol Records. He worked with many major jazz musicians there, including Frank Sinatra, Count Basie, Duke Ellington and Nat "King" Cole. But he became most known for refusing to release the first four singles of the Beatles, which he thought inappropriate for US audiences. Subsequently demoted, he returned to journalism, writing for *Billboard* magazine.

MICHAEL LEVIN was—along with Leonard Feather, Dave Dexter, and Nat Hentoff—one of the dominant columnists for *DownBeat Magazine* throughout the 1940s. However, in 1951 Levin left journalism to join an ad agency, and shortly thereafter developed "The Levin Plan" for Dwight Eisenhower's presidential campaign—a saturation of television spot advertising in swing states, the first extensive use of television in a presidential campaign.

DICK MACDOUGALL was a Canadian radio announcer who began in pop music radio—he was the first announcer on AM radio station CHUM. But he was best known for his work after that, hosting several popular radio interview programs on the CBC, before becoming the anchor of the seminal CBC television news/interview program *Tabloid.*

GEORGE WALSH was a long-time announcer, newscaster, and interviewer at KNX radio in Los Angeles, where he hosted a wide variety of programs, including a fashion show hosted by Edith Head, and a Peabody Award–winning overnight classical program. He was most famous for a side job at CBS, however, where he was known as the voice of *Gunsmoke*—introducing first the hit radio show and, later, the television version.

WILLIS CONOVER produced jazz concerts for TV and the movies, as well as at the White House and the Newport Jazz Festival. But he was best known for his forty-year stint hosting the *Voice of America Jazz Hour*, where he interviewed numerous jazz stars, including Benny Goodman and Stan Getz, and conducted what is thought to be the only in-depth interview of Art Tatum. The program made him a major celebrity in Eastern Europe and behind the Iron Curtain—although not in the United States, as the *VOA* was not broadcast domestically.

MIKE WALLACE was an American journalist particularly known for his hard-hitting interviews of newsmakers for the *60 Minutes* television show for thirty-seven years. Before that, he hosted numerous game shows and interview programs on local and syndicated television. Perhaps the best known of these was *Night Beat* and its follow-up, *The Mike Wallace Interview*, programs in which he interviewed a wide range of public figures, including Ayn Rand, Thurgood Marshall, the Imperial Wizard of the Ku Klux Klan (in full regalia), and numerous others.

THE LAST INTERVIEW SERIES

KURT VONNEGUT: THE LAST INTERVIEW

"I think it can be tremendously refreshing if a creator of literature has something on his mind other than the history of literature so far. Literature should not disappear up its own asshole, so to speak."

$15.95 / $17.95 CAN
978-1-61219-090-7
ebook: 978-1-61219-091-4

JACQUES DERRIDA: THE LAST INTERVIEW LEARNING TO LIVE FINALLY

"I am at war with myself, it's true, you couldn't possibly know to what extent... I say contradictory things that are, we might say, in real tension; they are what construct me, make me live, and will make me die."

translated by PASCAL-ANNE BRAULT and MICHAEL NAAS

$15.95 / $17.95 CAN
978-1-61219-094-5
ebook: 978-1-61219-032-7

ROBERTO BOLAÑO: THE LAST INTERVIEW

"Posthumous: It sounds like the name of a Roman gladiator, an unconquered gladiator. At least that's what poor Posthumous would like to believe. It gives him courage."

translated by SYBIL PEREZ and others

$15.95 / $17.95 CAN
978-1-61219-095-2
ebook: 978-1-61219-033-4

THE LAST INTERVIEW SERIES

JORGE LUIS BORGES: THE LAST INTERVIEW

"Believe me: the benefits of blindness have been greatly exaggerated. If I could see, I would never leave the house, I'd stay indoors reading the many books that surround me."

translated by KIT MAUDE

$15.95 / $15.95 CAN
978-1-61219-204-8
ebook: 978-1-61219-205-5

HANNAH ARENDT: THE LAST INTERVIEW

"There are no dangerous thoughts for the simple reason that thinking itself is such a dangerous enterprise."

$15.95 / $15.95 CAN
978-1-61219-311-3
ebook: 978-1-61219-312-0

RAY BRADBURY: THE LAST INTERVIEW

"You don't have to destroy books to destroy a culture. Just get people to stop reading them."

$15.95 / $15.95 CAN
978-1-61219-421-9
ebook: 978-1-61219-422-6

THE LAST INTERVIEW SERIES

JAMES BALDWIN: THE LAST INTERVIEW

"You don't realize that you're intelligent until it gets you into trouble."

$15.95 / $15.95 CAN
978-1-61219-400-4
ebook: 978-1-61219-401-1

GABRIEL GÁRCIA MÁRQUEZ: THE LAST INTERVIEW

"The only thing the Nobel Prize is good for is not having to wait in line."

$15.95 / $15.95 CAN
978-1-61219-480-6
ebook: 978-1-61219-481-3

LOU REED: THE LAST INTERVIEW

"Hubert Selby. William Burroughs. Allen Ginsberg. Delmore Schwartz... I thought if you could do what those writers did and put it to drums and guitar, you'd have the greatest thing on earth."

$15.95 / $15.95 CAN
978-1-61219-478-3
ebook: 978-1-61219-479-0

THE LAST INTERVIEW SERIES

ERNEST HEMINGWAY: THE LAST INTERVIEW

"The most essential gift for a good writer is a built-in, shockproof shit detector."

$15.95 / $20.95 CAN
978-1-61219-522-3
ebook: 978-1-61219-523-0

PHILIP K. DICK: THE LAST INTERVIEW

"The basic thing is, how frightened are you of chaos? And how happy are you with order?"

$15.95 / $20.95 CAN
978-1-61219-526-1
ebook: 978-1-61219-527-8

NORA EPHRON: THE LAST INTERVIEW

"You better *make* them care about what you think. It had better be quirky or perverse or thought-ful enough so that you hit some chord in them. Otherwise, it doesn't work."

$15.95 / $20.95 CAN
978-1-61219-524-7
ebook: 978-1-61219-525-4

THE LAST INTERVIEW SERIES

JANE JACOBS: THE LAST INTERVIEW

"I would like it to be understood that all our human economic achievements have been done by ordinary people, not by exceptionally educated people, or by elites, or by supernatural forces."

$15.95 / $20.95 CAN
978-1-61219-534-6
ebook: 978-1-61219-535-3

DAVID BOWIE: THE LAST INTERVIEW

"I have no time for glamour. It seems a ridiculous thing to strive for... A clean pair of shoes should serve quite well."

$16.99 / $22.99 CAN
978-1-61219-575-9
ebook: 978-1-61219-576-6

MARTIN LUTHER KING, JR.: THE LAST INTERVIEW

"Injustice anywhere is a threat to justice everywhere."

$15.99 / $21.99 CAN
978-1-61219-616-9
ebook: 978-1-61219-617-6

THE LAST INTERVIEW SERIES

CHRISTOPHER HITCHENS: THE LAST INTERVIEW

"If someone says I'm doing this out of faith, I say, Why don't you do it out of conviction?"

$15.99 / $20.99 CAN
978-1-61219-672-5
ebook: 978-1-61219-673-2

HUNTER S. THOMPSON: THE LAST INTERVIEW

"I feel in the mood to write a long weird story—a tale so strange and terrible that it will change the brain of the normal reader forever."

$15.99 / $20.99 CAN
978-1-61219-693-0
ebook: 978-1-61219-694-7

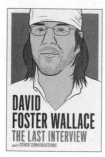

DAVID FOSTER WALLACE: THE LAST INTERVIEW AND OTHER CONVERSATIONS

"I'm a typical American. Half of me is dying to give myself away, and the other half is continually rebelling."

$16.99 / 21.99 CAN
978-1-61219-741-8
ebook: 978-1-61219-742-5

THE LAST INTERVIEW SERIES

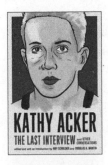

KATHY ACKER: THE LAST INTERVIEW AND OTHER CONVERSATIONS

"To my mind I was in a little cage in the zoo that instead of 'monkey' said 'female American radical.'"

$15.99 / $20.99 CAN
978-1-61219-731-9
ebook: 978-1-61219-732-6

PRINCE: THE LAST INTERVIEW AND OTHER CONVERSATIONS

"That's what you want. Transcendence. When that happens—oh, boy."

$16.99 / $22.99 CAN
978-1-61219-745-6
ebook: 978-1-61219-746-3

JULIA CHILD: THE LAST INTERVIEW AND OTHER CONVERSATIONS

"I'm not a chef, I'm a teacher and a cook."

$16.99 / $22.99 CAN
978-1-61219-733-3
ebook: 978-1-61219-734-0

THE LAST INTERVIEW SERIES

URSULA K. LE GUIN: THE LAST INTERVIEW AND OTHER CONVERSATIONS

"Resistance and change often begin in art.
Very often in our art, the art of words."

$16.99 / $21.99 CAN
978-1-61219-779-1
ebook: 978-1-61219-780-7